W9-AAZ-106

ACKNOWLEDGMENTS

*This book is the result
of your dedication, commitment, and support.
Thank you all so much for the
endless hours, energy, and creativity.
s.l.*

Ann George, my editor and co-writer, you are and have always been wonderful.
Thank you so much for all of your help. You're brilliant.

Linda Willemse, my assistant, whose help and devotion make it possible for me to do what I do

Nancy Berkoff, RD, EdD, CCE, food editor, who helped create many of the terrific recipes in this book

Norman Stewart, food stylist, "milk-mustache" man, and good friend, for your talent and creativity

DoHan Rogers, assistant food stylist extraordinaire, who was a pleasure to work with every day

Maryellen Baker, our fabulous photographer, who's demand for perfection helped create this work of art

Sawako Iizuka, photography assistant and rock 'n' roll aficionado, for your silent strength

Kimberly Hillman, Lisa Garza, and Anna Flanigan of inkfish, graphic designers, who brought my
vision to life and made it beautiful

Denise Betts, proofreader perfectionist, third eye and *Cheese Whiz*® spelling fanatic, for all of your
last minute help, as always it was invaluable

Kathy Talley-Jones, indexer and second set of eyes, for making "it" happen

CREDITS AND SOURCES

Room with a View, Santa Monica, CA   Pottery Barn   Banana Republic   Hear Music: Michael & Carmine

DEDICATION

This book is dedicated to my grandmother,
Lorraine Korth Waldroop,
whose love and guidance made me the person I am.
How fortunate I was to have you.
s.l.

SPECIAL THANKS

Bruce Karatz, my love, for your commitment and devotion; I am so thankful I've finally found you

Zane Rothschild, my mentor, whose little nudges along the way help me choose the right paths

Peggy and Bill Singlehurst, my auntie and unc, for your unconditional love and support

Kimber Lee, my sister, whose always been there for me or gone there for me, I love you

Cynthia Mark, my sister, for sharing your most precious creations so unselfishly

Rich and Paul (Johnny) Christiansen, my brothers, who I don't get to cook for enough,
I'm so proud of both of you

Lee Gaskill and Michele Christiansen, for being such wonderful additions to our family

Danielle, Austen, Taner, Scottie, Stephanie, Bryce, Brandon, and Blake, my nieces and nephews,
who are sweeter than any dessert I could ever make

Aspen, my baby dog, who owns my heart and is the most human being I know

Colleen Schmidt, my best friend, who since college has been like a sister to me; to all the
corn dogs, root beer floats, dreams, and confidences

Lisa Kridos, Dan Strone, Dick Clark, Harvey Mackay, Rick Frishman, David Hahn,
Jack Canfield, Bob Karatz, who have inspired me and advised me — thank you

5

Table of Contents

Semi-Homemade Cooking will make your life much easier than it's ever been before! I've spent the past ten years creating a Semi-Homemade Lifestyle for myself — and now for you — busy people on a budget and on the go. Our days are filled with too much to do, too little time to do it in, and not enough money to make "it" all happen. Whether we are corporate divas or domestic goddesses, life requires us all to be super-human. "To-do" lists have gone from one-page handwritten sheets to entire chapters in a hardbound book. And after getting all your "to-dos" done, you're expected to plan, shop for, and whip up new, fresh, mouth-watering homemade meals from scratch? Please!

What is Semi-Homemade Cooking? It's a new way of cooking where nothing is made from scratch anymore. The Semi-Homemade Cooking approach is easily done by combining several pre-packaged foods, a few fresh ingredients, and a "pinch of this with a hint of that" to make new, easy, gourmet-tasting, and inexpensive meals in minutes. It's fast, fabulous food.

How will Semi-Homemade Cooking make your life easier? Each recipe comes complete with time estimates for planning, cost guidelines for budgeting, and a suggested name-brand list of ingredients to ease your shopping load. So whether you are cooking for two or twenty, there will always be something easy, quick, and affordable to prepare. You'll be the "Julia Child" of your own kitchen without the time, energy, and expense it normally requires.

What will you get here that you can't get any other place? You'll get an entirely new way of cooking. You'll get recipes that anyone can do. You'll get the benefit of quality and taste without the stress traditional cooking creates.

I'd love to hear any thoughts, ideas, questions, or suggestions you may have. Welcome to a new Semi-Homemade world.

brand names

Stylish, quality cooking is made easy when using our pre-selected and tested brand names. These

pre-combined ingredient sources reduce expenses and enhance taste. Substitutions, of course, are

always at your discretion. Brand-name suggestions are highlighted throughout each recipe in italics.

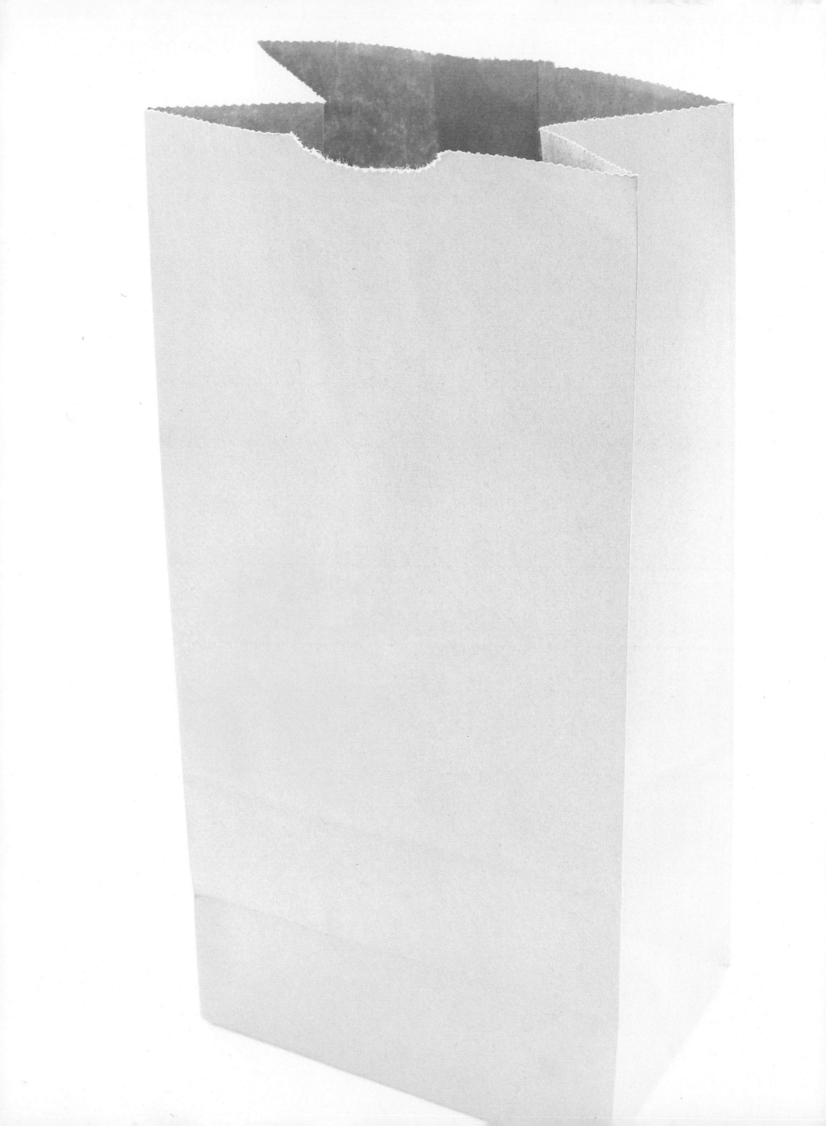

budget

BUDGET

Even when on a budget, there is no need to sacrifice the quality or quantity of your food. With so

much to choose from, in all price ranges, budgets can be easy to accommodate with a little know-how.

The $ signs shown with each recipe will give you a guideline of the cost per serving.

$ Inexpensive $$ Low Cost $$$ Medium Cost $$$$ Expensive

prepping, cooking, cooling

PREPPING, COOKING, AND COOLING TIMES

Time is on your side. Each quick, easy recipe comes complete with time estimates. You decide how

much time you have to spend in your kitchen. A new luxury you're sure to appreciate and enjoy.

suggested wines

SUGGESTED WINES

A good wine, whether expensive or not, warms the way to ending a day. It's a palate-pleaser before,

during, or after dinner. A relaxing way to enjoy a weekend lunch or an afternoon brunch. Try the suggested

wines, and soon you too will feel as knowledgeable as any connoisseur.

MUSIC SELECTION

Music sets a mood and creates an ambience. It can mellow you out, lift you up, or get you going.

It can remind you of past memories and create new ones. Music selections are shared in most of the

chapters. So throughout your busy day, remember to "hear the music."

disposables

DISPOSABLES

Making life easier can be so simple if you utilize disposable products. With quick clean-up and neatly

organized food storage, you'll minimize your work while maximizing your leisure time.

BREAKFAST

Breakfast, as they say, is the most important meal of the day. This may be true, but try to convince yourself to sit down for five minutes and eat when you're running late, not hungry, and can't even see straight. Growing up, I was fine with *Captain Crunch®* and milk — that much sugar will give anyone plenty of energy, for a while. But the nutritional value, or lack thereof, will send your energy crashing way before lunchtime. Still, I must admit, a sugar-filled cereal breakfast of *Captain Crunch®* is better than no breakfast at all.

Without breakfast, you can feel exhausted after a great night's sleep. You can find yourself becoming easily irritable and have difficulty concentrating. Having a bad morning, or even a bad day, cannot always be blamed on waking up on the wrong side of the bed, rather it's trying to function properly and at full capacity without giving your body what it needs: fuel.

This chapter is filled with delicious, simple breakfast choices that will quickly jump-start your day. Some are sugar-filled (because I couldn't resist), and most can be prepared the night before and re-heated the next day to make your precious morning moments even more manageable.

CREPES BENEDICT

Serves 2

4   slices turkey bacon, *Hormel®*
2   10" pre-made crepes, *Mrs. Frieda®*
4   eggs
2   tablespoons butter, *Land O Lakes®*
1   8-ounce can of hollandaise sauce, *Aunt Penny's®*
      salt
      pepper

Prep Time: 5 minutes
Cooking Time: 8 minutes

Preparation:

Prepare bacon according to package instructions. Place crepes in plastic wrap and heat in microwave for 20 seconds. Whisk eggs in a bowl. On medium heat, melt 2 tablespoons of butter in a skillet. Add eggs and stir constantly until light and fluffy. Sprinkle with salt and pepper. Place hollandaise sauce in a cup and microwave for approximately 35 seconds, then set aside. On each breakfast plate, put one crepe. Place half the scrambled eggs and 2 slices of the bacon in the center. Roll up, enchilada-style. Top with 2 tablespoons of hollandaise sauce. Serve immediately.

$$

Music Selection: *Natalie MacMaster, "In My Hands"*

FRENCH APPLE RAISIN SANDWICHES

Serves 2

2   eggs
$1/4$ cup milk
$1/4$ teaspoon ground cinnamon, *McCormick*®
4   slices raisin bread, *Wonder*®
1   5-ounce can apple pie filling divided into two equal portions, *Comstock*®
1   tablespoon butter, *Land O Lakes*®
1   tablespoon powdered sugar, *C&H*®

Prep Time: 5 minutes
Cooking Time: 8 minutes

Preparation:

In a medium bowl, combine eggs, milk, and cinnamon. Set aside. Create 2 sandwiches with the bread and apple pie filling. Place sandwiches in a flat pan, and pour egg mixture over top — let soak for 2 minutes. Egg should be absorbed into bread completely. In a large skillet, over medium heat, melt the butter. Place each sandwich into the skillet. Cook approximately 4 minutes on each side or until browned. Cut into halves, garnish with sprinkled powder sugar. Serve with maple syrup if desired.

$$

$$ Music Selection: *Dori Caymmi, "Self-Titled"*

HUEVOS RANCHEROS

Serves 2

1	14-ounce can low-fat black beans, *Del Monte®*
1	tablespoon diced green chilis, *Las Palmas®*
1/4	cup salsa, drained, *Pace®*
1	tablespoon chopped cilantro
2	flour tortillas, *El Paso®*
4	eggs
2	tablespoons shredded cheddar cheese, *Sargento®*
1	green onion, sliced thinly

Prep Time: 5 minutes
Cooking Time: 10 minutes

Preparation:

Preheat oven to 400 degrees. In a medium saucepan, on medium heat, combine beans, green chilis, drained salsa, and cilantro. Simmer for 4 minutes, stirring occasionally. Remove from heat. Cut tortillas into shapes using cookie cutters and place on a foil-covered baking sheet. Bake until slightly browned. Cook eggs sunnyside up or over medium.

Place 1 cup of the bean mixture onto each plate. Put 2 eggs next to the beans. Arrange the tortillas around the dish and garnish with the green onions and shredded cheese. If desired, top with a dollop of sour cream. Serve immediately.

$$ Music Selection: *Loreena McKennitt, "The Book of Secrets"*

MORNING GLORY FONDUE

Serves 4

1	cup champagne, *Cook's*®
2	cups cream cheese, *Philadelphia*®
1	cup sour cream
1	teaspoon mustard, *French's*®
2	tablespoons flour, *Pillsbury*®
1	cup smoked salmon, *Lasco*®
3	small tomatoes, chunks
3	hard-boiled eggs, chunks
1	package English muffins, *Thomas'*®
4	bagels (plain, water, or egg)

Prep Time: 7 minutes
Cooking Time: 10 minutes

Preparation:

In a medium saucepan, on medium-high heat, add champagne and bring to a quick boil. Reduce heat to medium-low. In a small bowl, combine cream cheese, sour cream, mustard, flour, salmon, tomatoes, and hard-boiled eggs. Slowly (about a $^1/_2$ cup at a time) add cheese mixture to champagne, stirring until all cheese is melted and mixture is blended. Serve bubbly hot. Cut English muffins and bagels into 1" chunks and dip into fondue.

$$ Music Selection: *Passion Planet, Various Artists, "Songs of Love from Around the World"*

PUMPKIN CINNAMON PANCAKES

Serves 2

Pancake Ingredients:
1	cup pancake mix, *Krusteaz®*
3/4	cup cold water
1	15-ounce can pumpkin, *Libby's®*
1/8	teaspoon cinnamon, *McCormick®*
1/8	teaspoon ground ginger, *McCormick®*

Syrup Ingredients:
4	tablespoons plus 1 tablespoon chopped pecans, *Diamond®*
2	cups butter pecan-flavored maple syrup, *Blackburn's®*

Prep Time:	5 minutes
Cooking Time:	4 minutes

Preparation:

In a medium bowl, combine pancake mix, water, pumpkin, 2 tablespoons pecans, cinnamon, and ginger. Set aside. In a microwave-proof bowl, add 2 tablespoons pecans to syrup and microwave for 25 seconds on medium. Preheat a flat grill or nonstick skillet to medium. Place several tablespoons of batter in the heated skillet to make each pancake. Cook for 2 minutes or until bubbles appear, then turn over and cook for an additional 2 minutes. Top with butter, serve with warmed pecan syrup and garnish with remaining pecans.

$$ Music Selection: *Ella Fitzgerald, "Priceless Jazz Collection"*

ENGLISH CROWN SCRAMBLE

Serves 6

6   puff pastry shells, *Pepperidge Farms*®
6   eggs, slightly beaten
1/4 cup milk
1   tablespoon butter, *Land O Lakes*®
1   teaspoon vegetable oil, *Wesson*®
     salt
     pepper

MORNAY SAUCE:

1   tablespoon butter, *Land O Lakes*®
1   tablespoon all-purpose flour, *Pillsbury*®
2/3 cup water
2/3 cup powdered milk, *Carnation*®
1/4 cup shredded Swiss cheese, *Sargento*®
3   tablespoons shredded parmesan, *Sargento*®

Prep Time: 3 minutes
Cooking Time: 12 minutes

Preparation:

Preheat oven to 400 degrees. Place the puff pastry shells on a baking sheet and bake for 12 minutes or until golden on top. While pastries are baking, melt butter in a medium saucepan over medium heat. Add the flour and whisk into a paste. Add water, powdered milk, Swiss cheese, and parmesan cheese. Bring to a simmer, set aside. In a 10-inch skillet over medium heat, add oil and butter. In a medium bowl, beat together milk and eggs. When the butter foams, add in the egg mixture. Stir continuously (approximately 2 minutes) until eggs are light and fluffy. Season with salt and pepper. Hollow out each pastry crown and fill with 1/4 cup scrambled eggs and top with 2 to 3 tablespoons of Mornay sauce.

$$

Music Selection: *Dee Carstensen, "Regarding the Soul"*

COUNTRY BISCUITS & GRAVY

Serves 2

1	container prepared biscuits, *Pillsbury Grands*®
4	ounces pork sausage, *Jimmy Dean*®
1	tablespoon all-purpose flour, *Pillsbury*®
1	10-ounce can of white sauce, *Aunt Penny's*®
1	cup milk

Prep Time: 5 minutes
Cooking Time: 12 minutes

Preparation:

Bake 2 biscuits from the container according to package instructions and save the rest in a storage container in the refrigerator. In a small skillet, over medium heat, sauté sausage until cooked thoroughly. Sprinkle flour over sausage and stir, cook for 2 additional minutes. Add white sauce and milk to sausage mixture and bring to a simmer. Remove from heat. Cut biscuits in half and place 2 halves on each plate. Spoon sausage gravy generously over the top of each biscuit half and serve hot.

$$ Music Selection: *Catie Curtis, "Truth from Lies"*

DATE CARROT MUFFINS

Makes 12 muffins

1   package (1 pound) plain muffin mix, *Pillsbury*®
1   cup bran
1   egg
1   cup milk
1   cup shredded carrots, *Mann's*®
1   cup pitted dates, chopped (dates may be available already chopped), *Dromedary*®

Prep Time: 4 minutes
Cooking Time: 20 minutes

Preparation:

Preheat oven to 400 degrees. Line muffin tins with muffin papers or spray with *Pam*®. In medium bowl, combine (do not over-mix) muffin mix, bran, egg, and milk. Fold in carrots and dates. The batter will be lumpy. Fill each muffin tin approximately 2/3 full and bake for 20 minutes or until centers of muffins are cooked thoroughly.

$

Music Selection: *Carrie Newcomer, "Visions and Dreams"*

EGGS IN A NEST

Serves 4

6   large eggs
1   teaspoon black pepper, *McCormick®*
1   teaspoon seasoned salt, *Lawry's®*
2   tablespoons butter, *Land O Lakes®*
4   slices whole wheat bread, *Wonder®*
8   teaspoons Cheese Whiz, *Kraft®*
    vegetable oil spray, *Pam®*

Prep Time: 5 minutes
Cooking Time: 7 minutes

Preparation:

Preheat oven to 325 degrees. Place a 10" skillet over medium heat. Spray 4 oven-proof custard or dessert cups with *Pam®*. In a small bowl, beat eggs with pepper and seasoned salt until foamy. Melt butter in skillet; once melted add egg mixture and stir constantly for approximately 2 minutes, or until eggs are light and fluffy. Place 1 slice of bread in each cup and mold to fit. Spread bread with butter or margarine — this prevents eggs from making the bread soggy. Place 1 teaspoon of *Cheese Whiz®* in the bottom of each piece of bread. Equally divide eggs into the 4 breaded *Cheese Whiz®* cups. Spoon 1 teaspoon of *Cheese Whiz®* over each of the egg tops. Bake for 5 minutes until cheese is melted.

Garnish: Shredded cheese and chopped tomatoes, if desired.

$

Music Selection: *Tracy Chapman, "Telling Stories"*

CRISPY RICE PUDDING

Serves 2

2   3.5-ounce vanilla pudding cups, *Kozy Shack*®
3   teaspoons golden raisins, *Dole*®
1   teaspoon ground cinnamon, *McCormick*®
1   cup Rice Krispies, *Kellogg's*®

Prep Time: 3 minutes

Preparation:

Place the contents of each pudding cup into a separate serving dish. In a medium bowl, combine raisins, cinnamon, and *Rice Krispies*®. Evenly spoon raisin mixture over the pudding and serve immediately. Top with additional *Rice Krispies*®, if desired.

$

Music Selection: *Enya, "A Day Without Rain"*

STRAWBERRY BANANA BREAD PUDDING

Serves 10

1	box banana bread mix, *Pillsbury®*
2	eggs
2	tablespoons oil, *Wesson®*
1/3	cup apple juice, *Mott's®*
1	cup strawberry jam, *Welch's®*
1	cup water

Prep Time: 5 minutes
Cooking Time: 45 minutes
Cooling Time: 15 minutes

Preparation:

Preheat oven to 375 degrees. Grease and flour the bottom and sides of a large baking dish. Set aside. In a large bowl, combine banana bread mix, 2 eggs, oil, apple juice, and strawberry jam; mix thoroughly. Pour into floured baking pan and bake for 45 minutes or until a butter knife inserted into center of bread comes out clean. Cool for 15 minutes.

STRAWBERRY TOPPING

2	cups frozen strawberries, thawed
1	cup apple juice concentrate, thawed, *Mott's®*
1	cup mixed berry yogurt, *Dannon®*

In a medium bowl, slightly crush strawberries. Add apple juice concentrate and yogurt and mix for a thick sauce. Spoon on bread pudding after it has cooled (or right before eating).

$$

Music Selection: *Tasmin Archer, "Great Expectations"*

LUNCH

Lighter, smaller portions eaten at noon can be as appetizing and satisfying as dinner. Lunches shared with co-workers, friends, or family are always a mid-day delight. Looking back on my childhood, one of the highlights of my day was the delectable surprise awaiting me at lunchtime. Little did I know how necessary lunch is to maintaining a healthy attitude and high energy level. Now, lunch is about taking a little personal time to enjoy a meal, catch up, and catch my breath.

Often, lunch can seem uneventful and humdrum, especially when it's the same old selection in the fridge, or when there is nothing appealing at the local restaurants, delis, or fast-food chains. Semi-Homemade lunches will entice the pickiest of palates, and put the pizzazz back into your noon-day breaks. You will find recipes suitable for weekdays or weekends, intimate lunches, or playtime pow-wows.

Whether you want to eat light, are feeling famished, or just want something healthy to nosh on, there is so much here to choose from. Best of all, each recipe is quick to make and always tastes great whether eaten at home or at the office.

PEPPER PEACH CHICKEN SKEWER

Makes 24 pieces

2 teaspoons olive oil, *Star®*
2 teaspoons lemon juice, *ReaLemon®*
2 teaspoons fresh crushed garlic
1 teaspoon cumin, *McCormick®*
5 chicken breasts, cleaned and cut into 1-inch cubes
1 bag frozen peaches, thawed and cubed
  salt
  pepper

Prep Time: 20 minutes
Cooking Time: 10 minutes

Preparation:

Preheat oven to 375 degrees. In a medium bowl, combine olive oil, lemon juice, garlic, and cumin to create marinade. Place chicken breast cubes into marinade and refrigerate for 20 minutes. On toothpicks, skewer a chicken cube and a peach cube. Sprinkle with salt and pepper. Place on a foil-covered baking sheet. Roast for 10 minutes, until cooked thoroughly. Serve hot.

$$ Music Selection: *Afro Celt Sound System, Volume 2: Release, "Fire Under: World Dance"*

BLACK BEAN QUESADILLA

Serves 2

2   large flour tortillas, *El Paso®*
1   cup refried black beans, *Rosarito®*
1   cup medium salsa, *Pace® Thick 'n Chunky*
1   cup Mexican-style shredded cheese, *Sargento®*
1   cup guacamole (refrigerated section), *Deans®*
2   tablespoons sour cream

Prep Time: 5 minutes
Cooking Time: 10 minutes

Preparation:

Preheat oven to 400 degrees. Lay a tortilla on a clean surface. Spread the refried beans evenly over the tortilla. Spread the salsa over the beans (be sure to keep some salsa for your topping). Sprinkle the cheese over the beans and salsa and top with the second tortilla. Place the quesadilla on a foil-covered baking sheet. Bake for approximately 10 minutes or until the top is browned and the cheese is melted. While the quesadilla is baking, combine the guacamole and the sour cream in a small bowl. Cut the quesadilla into four equal portions and serve on a plate with a spoonful of the guacamole sauce and salsa.

$$

Music Selection: *Sting, "Brand New Day"*

SOUTHWESTERN TURKEY CHILI & CORNBREAD

Serves 2

CORNBREAD:

1   box cornbread mix, *Jiffy®*
1   11-ounce can Mexicorn, drained, *Green Giant®*
1¼ cups water

Prep Time: 3 minutes
Cooking Time: 25 minutes

Preparation:

Preheat oven to 400 degrees. In a medium bowl, combine cornbread mix, drained Mexicorn, and water. Stir until smooth. Spray 8x8x2-inch pan with nonstick spray. Fold mix into pan and bake for 25 minutes or until center is cooked thoroughly. While baking, prepare chili.

CHILI:

1   15-ounce can spicy black bean chili, *Healthy Valley®*
1   14-ounce can stewed tomatoes, Mexican recipe style, *Del Monte®*
10 ounces ground turkey
1   tablespoon all-purpose flour, *Pillsbury®*
1   teaspoon olive oil, *Star®*

Preparation:

In a *Ziploc®* bag, combine the flour and ground turkey and shake until the flour is absorbed into the meat. In a saucepan, on medium heat, sauté the turkey in the olive oil until browned. Add tomatoes and canned chili, simmer for 5–10 minutes. Chili should be slightly thick. Serve hot with cornbread.

$$$ Music Selection: *Spinners, "The Best of the Spinners"*

GNOCCHI DIPPERS

Serves 4

1   9-ounce package gnocchi (dry pasta section), *Alessi®*
      or substitute with cheese tortellini pasta, *Rosetto's®*

SAUCE:

1/4   brown onion, minced
1   teaspoon olive oil, *Star®*
1/4   cup reduced fat milk
1/4   teaspoon *Tabasco®*
1   cup Velveeta cheese, *Kraft®*
2   tablespoons non-fat sour cream

Prep Time: 4 minutes
Cooking Time: 10 minutes

Preparation:

Prepare the gnocchi according to package instructions.

In a medium saucepan, on medium heat, sauté onion in the olive oil for approximately 2 minutes. Add remaining ingredients — milk, *Tabasco®*, and cheese. Stir until sauce is smooth and cheese has completely melted. Fold gnocchi into the sauce. Top with sour cream. Serve immediately!

Note: Packaged sauce mixes can be used in place of the Velveeta®, prepared according to package instructions.

$$

Music Selection: *Les Nubians, "Princesses Nubiennes"*

TAHITIAN SALAD

Serves 4

3	cups ready-to-eat turkey breast, cubed, *Louis Rich*®
1	cup frozen chopped bell pepper, thawed, *Green Giant*®
2	teaspoons curry powder, *McCormick*®
1	teaspoon ginger, *McCormick*®
1	cup mayonnaise, *Best Foods*®
2	tablespoons prepared chutney
1	15-ounce can drained tropical fruit cocktail, *Dole*®
1/8	cup sesame seeds, *McCormick*®
1	cup shredded coconut, *Snowflake*®
5	romaine lettuce leaves
1	11-ounce can drained Mandarin oranges, *Del Monte*®

Prep Time: 10 minutes

Preparation:

In a medium bowl, combine cubed turkey, chopped pepper, curry, ginger, mayonnaise, chutney, and drained fruit cocktail until mixed. Sprinkle in sesame seeds and coconut. Place lettuce leaves on individual serving plates, top with turkey mixture and garnish with Mandarin oranges.

$$

Music Selection: *Robert Miles, "Dreamland"*

PROSCIUTTO & GOAT CHEESE PIZZA

Serves 2

1	package pizza shell with sauce, *Boboli®*
1	cup shredded mozzarella, *Sargento®*
4	ounces prosciutto (deli section), *Citterio®*
2	tablespoons fresh basil, chopped
1	ounce goat cheese

Prep Time: 6 minutes
Cooking Time: 12 minutes

Preparation:

Preheat oven to 425 degrees. On a foil-covered pizza or baking sheet, lay *Boboli®* pizza shell. Spread sauce evenly over the *Boboli®*. Cover with mozzarella cheese. Add prosciutto, chopped basil, and dots of goat cheese to the top of mozzarella and bake for approximately 12 minutes. Prosciutto will be crisp and the cheese melted evenly when done. Cut into 6 even slices.

$$$ Music Selection: *Martin Sexton, "The American"*

CURRIED BOWTIE SALAD

Serves 4

1   8-ounce package fresh bowtie noodles, *Celentano's*®
1   ripe medium avocado, peeled and sliced
1   medium red apple, diced
1   15-ounce can pineapple chunks, drained, *Dole*®
1   cup sour cream
2   teaspoons curry powder, *McCormick*®

Prep Time: 10 minutes
Set-up Time: 15 minutes

Preparation:

In a medium pot, bring 4 cups of water to a boil. Add bowtie noodles and cook for approximately three minutes. Strain and allow to cool. In a large bowl, mix peeled and sliced avocado, diced apple, drained pineapple chunks, sour cream and curry powder. Fold in noodles. Place in refrigerator and allow to chill for 15 minutes before serving.

Suggestion: Salad can be served on a bed of shredded red cabbage or on fresh baby spinach.

$$ \quad $$

$$

Music Selection: *Doobie Brothers, "Best of the Doobies"*

BEEFY STEW

Serves 2

1   sheet puff pastry, cut two 4-inch rounds, *Pepperidge Farm®*
1   tablespoon all-purpose flour, *Pillsbury®*
1   teaspoon olive oil, *Star®*
1   15-ounce can country vegetable soup, *Campbell's®*
10   ounces stew meat, cubed

Prep Time: 5 minutes
Cooking Time: 13 minutes

Preparation:

Preheat oven to 425 degrees. Bake the two cut puff pastries approximately 10–12 minutes or until pastry is slightly browned on top and baked thoroughly. While baking, in a *Ziploc®* bag, combine meat and flour until flour is absorbed. In a saucepan, over medium heat, sauté the meat in olive oil until slightly browned (approximately 6–8 minutes). Add vegetable soup and simmer for approximately 5 minutes or until slightly thickened. Pour stew equally into 2 bowls and top each with a pastry dough round.

$$

$$

$$ $$

\$\$ Music Selection: *Faire Celts, Various Artists, "A Woman's Voice"*

SALAD CHINOIS

Serves 4

1   12.5-ounce can chicken breast chunks, drained and cubed, *Tyson®*
1   cup cole slaw mix (shredded cabbage and carrots, without sauce), *Mann's®*
2   8-ounce cans chow mein vegetables, drained, *Chun King®*
1   5-ounce bag prepared green salad, *Fresh Express®*
1   5-ounce can chow mein noodles, *La Choy®*
1   11-ounce can Mandarin orange segments, drained, *Dole®*

DRESSING

1   cup mayonnaise, *Best Foods®*
2   tablespoons soy sauce, *Kikkoman®*
1   teaspoon ground ginger, *McCormick®*

Prep Time: 10 minutes

Preparation:

In a medium bowl, toss chicken, cole slaw mix, and drained chow mein vegetables until well mixed. In a small bowl, mix mayonnaise, soy sauce, and ginger for your dressing. To assemble salads, line individual bowls or plates with a small amount of green salad, place chicken, chow mein, and slaw mixture on top of salad, spoon dressing on top of chicken. Garnish with noodles and Mandarin orange segments.

Serve with fresh melon skewers or sliced fresh pineapple.

$$

Music Selection: *Madonna, "Ray of Light"*

FOUR-CHEESE TORTELLINI

Serves 4

1	jar *Cheese Whiz, Kraft*®
1	cup milk
1	tablespoon butter, *Land O Lakes*®
1	teaspoon *Tabasco*® sauce
2	cups *Sargento*® *Four Cheese Pizza Blend* (mozzarella, cheddar, parmesan, jack)
1	9-ounce package fresh mixed cheese tortellini (refrigerated section), *Rosetto's*®

Prep Time: 10 minutes
Cooking Time: 15 minutes

Preparation:

Preheat oven to 350 degrees. In a large saucepan, over low heat, combine *Cheese Whiz*® and milk, stir until melted and smooth. Add butter, *Tabasco*®, and cheese. Stir until cheese is melted and mixture is smooth. In a large baking dish, place tortellini and sauce. Bake for approximately 15 minutes or until bubbly. Serve hot.

$$ Music Selection: *Everything But The Girl, "Walking Wounded"*

CRAB ASPARAGUS AU GRATIN

Serves 4

1   package potatoes au gratin, *Betty Crocker*®
1   cup shredded cheddar cheese, *Sargento*®
1   cup milk
1   cup frozen cut asparagus, thawed, *Green Giant*®
1   4.25-ounce can crabmeat, rinsed and drained, *Starkist*®

Prep Time: 15 minutes
Cooking Time: 15 minutes

Preparation:

Preheat oven to 350 degrees. Prepare potatoes according to package instructions. In a large saucepan, heat cheese and milk, stirring, until cheese is melted. Add potatoes, thawed asparagus, and drained crabmeat until mixture is hot. Place in large baking pan and bake for 15 minutes or until top is golden brown.

$$

Music Selection: *John Williams, "Greatest Hits 1969–1999"*

DINNER

Dinner should be seen as a celebration that ends another productive day. It's a time to reflect and share ideas, new happenings, and current events. It's also a time for you and yours to relax and unwind, a time for families to bond and communicate while reinforcing the security and stability of home. Dinner should be a pleasure — a time to laugh, have fun, and enjoy each other's company. It shouldn't be yet another stressful "to-do" on your list. Preparing dinner can be easy and satisfying with Semi-Homemade recipes.

Many of us have dinner on the run. For you domestic goddesses, bad habits are easily formed when constantly trying to squeeze your families' dinner in between soccer practice, homework, and last-minute errands. For you corporate divas, take-out and eating at your desk is commonplace when trying to meet demanding deadlines. Regardless, both scenarios are unhealthy and rob everyone of the important downtime and the pleasure of a good meal. Semi-Homemade dinners are simple to make and give you more time to enjoy yourself and others without sacrificing taste or nutrition.
Bon appetit!

DIJON CHICKEN & MUSHROOMS

Serves 4

4	chicken breasts, skinned and cleaned
1	tomato, diced
1	15-ounce can corn niblets, *Green Giant®*

SAUCE:

2	tablespoons dijon mustard, *Heinz®*
1	10-ounce can *Condensed Fat-free Cream of Mushroom Soup, Campbell's®*
1	10-ounce can non-fat milk (or one soup can full)
1	package alfredo sauce mix, *Schilling®*
12	chopped mushrooms

Prep Time:	7 minutes
Cooking Time:	30 minutes

Preparation:

Preheat oven to 400 degrees. In a small bowl, whisk with a fork, mustard, cream of mushroom soup, milk, and alfredo sauce mix until smooth. Add chopped mushrooms. Place chicken breasts in a pie pan. Cover chicken with sauce. Bake for 20–25 minutes or until chicken is cooked through. Garnish with diced tomatoes and corn niblets. May be served with yellow rice.

$$ Suggested Wine: *Blue Nun® Chardonnay*   Music Selection: *Etta James, "At Last"*

73

STEAK PINWHEELS WITH SUNDRIED TOMATO STUFFING

Serves 4

1   package stuffing, *Stove Top*® (flavor optional)
1   14-ounce can beef stock, *Swanson*®
1   cup ready-to-use julienne sundried tomatoes, *Frieda's*®
1   pound skirt steak, cleaned

Prep Time: 10 minutes
Cooking Time: 45 minutes

Preparation:

Preheat oven to 400 degrees. Prepare the stuffing according to package instructions, substituting beef stock for water. Add the sundried tomatoes halfway through the cooking process. Once stuffing is cooked, lay the skirt steak out onto a clean flat surface. Spread stuffing evenly over the skirt steak and roll to create a pinwheel effect, secure it with toothpicks. Place the roll on a foil-covered baking sheet and roast for approximately 30–45 minutes or until cooked thoroughly.

ROSEMARY MASHED POTATOES

2   teaspoons fresh rosemary, chopped
1   package *mashed potatoes, Simply Potatoes*®
    salt

Prep Time: 2 minutes
Cooking Time: 5 minutes

Preparation:

Peel corner on *Simply Potatoes*® to remove cover. Warm potatoes according to package instructions with 1 tablespoon butter and 1 tablespoon milk. Add in rosemary and salt. Serve hot. May be served with our "More than Meatloaf" gravy (recipe found in GRAVIES & SAUCES chapter).

$$$ Suggested Wine: *Kendall Jackson*® *Cabernet Sauvignon*
             Music Selection: *Hi Fidelity Lounge, Various Artists "Volume 1: Subterranean Soundtracks"*

MEATY MICROWAVE LASAGNA

Serves 6

1	8-ounce package lasagna noodles, *Ronzoni®*
1	pound ground beef
1	1.37-ounce package spaghetti sauce mix, *French's®*
1	15-ounce can tomato sauce, *Classico®*
1	cup small curd cottage cheese
3	5-ounce package sliced mozzarella cheese, *Sargento®*
1	cup shredded parmesan cheese, *Sargento®*
1	loaf frozen garlic bread, *Momma Bella®*

Prep Time: 15 minutes
Cooking Time: 25 minutes
Cooling Time: 5 minutes

Preparation:

In a microwave-safe 2-quart baking dish, place noodles and cover with water. Microwave on high for 10 minutes. Remove from microwave and let stand (in water). Brown ground beef in a frying pan and drain, discard fat. In a medium bowl, mix ground meat, spaghetti sauce mix, and tomato sauce. Microwave on medium for 3 minutes. Drain noodles.

To form lasagna: repeatedly layer noodles, ground beef sauce, cottage cheese, mozzarella, and parmesan cheese (in that order) in microwave-safe dish (the same used for the noodles). Be sure to use layering ingredients sparingly in order to make 4 layers minimum. Last layer should be meat sauce and cheeses. Sprinkle the top of lasagna with water. Microwave on medium for 10 minutes or until lasagna is thoroughly heated. Let cool for 5 minutes before cutting. This can be assembled ahead of time and refrigerated until ready to microwave. Cooked lasagna may be frozen.

ONE LOAF GARLIC BREAD

Prepare according to package instructions.

$$$ Suggested Wine: *BV® Merlot*   Music Selection: *Francis Albert Sinatra & Antonio Carlos Jobim*

SHANGRI-LA LOBSTER WITH CRISPY SPINACH

Serves 4

4	4-ounce lobster tails
2	tablespoons all-purpose flour, *Pillsbury®*
2	teaspoons *Chef Paul's® Magic Seafood Seasoned Blend*
I	tablespoon olive oil, *Star®*
I	box lemon-flavored herb jasmine rice, *Knorr®*
I	8-ounce can golden curry sauce, *S & B®* (international food section)
I	cup water
I	8-ounce jar applesauce, *Mott's®*
I	cup coconut milk (Asian section of grocery store)
I	cup fat-free chicken stock, *Swanson®*
2	bunches spinach leaves
2	cups pure vegetable oil, *Wesson®*
	salt

Prep Time: 15 minutes
Cooking Time: 20 minutes

Preparation:

Remove lobster tails from shell and wash. In a medium-size pot with 4 cups of water, boil tail shells for 2–3 minutes until shell is bright red for dinner presentation.

Prepare rice according to package instructions. Set aside.

Curry Sauce: In a medium saucepan, over medium heat, add curry sauce and I cup of water. Add 8 ounces *Mott's®* applesauce, I cup coconut milk, and I cup chicken stock. Bring to a boil, set aside.

Crispy Spinach: Wash spinach leaves, cut off stems and dry them well. In a large skillet, over medium-high heat, place 2 cups *Wesson®* pure vegetable oil. The oil must be hot in order to ensure best results. To test: Add I leaf to the hot oil. If leaf begins to fry immediately, you are ready to start the cooking process. Add spinach and fry until crisp and translucent. Be careful not to get splattered. Remove leaves onto paper towels to drain. The spinach should have a jade green color. Salt to taste.

Lobster: Mix 2 tablespoons all-purpose flour and 2 teaspoons *Chef Paul's® Magic Seafood Seasoned Blend,* together in a *Ziploc®* bag. Add lobster tails, shake until coated. Place I tablespoon olive oil onto medium skillet over medium high heat. Once the oil is hot, place lobster into skillet and cover. Cook approximately 2^1/$_2$ minutes on each side or until cooked thoroughly yet moist and tender.

Presentation:

On each plate, add I cup rice, place a lobster tail on the side of rice and fill the open space left with crispy spinach. Drizzle with curry sauce and garnish with lobster shell.

$$$$ Suggested Wine: *Bendange® Chardonnay*   Music Selection: *Count Basie, "Trust Your Instincts"*

LEMON TURKEY CUTLETS

Serves 4

1	package (about 1 1/4 pounds) refrigerated boneless turkey cutlets, *The Turkey Store*®
1/3	cup vegetable oil, *Wesson*®
1/3	cup white flour, *Pillsbury*®
1	egg, beaten
2	tablespoons lemon juice, *ReaLemon*®
1	cup seasoned breadcrumbs, *Progresso*®
3	tablespoons chopped onions, fresh

Prep Time: 7 minutes
Cooking Time: 10 minutes

Preparation:

Rinse cutlets with cold water and pat dry with paper towels. Place flour in a medium bowl. In a second medium bowl, combine egg and lemon juice. In a third medium bowl, combine breadcrumbs and onions. In a large skillet, on medium-high heat, warm oil. While oil is heating, dip each cutlet in egg, then flour, and then breadcrumbs. Place cutlets in hot oil and cook until browned, about 4–5 minutes on each side. Serve hot. May be served with our "Lemon Mustard" sauce (recipe found in GRAVIES & SAUCES chapter).

$$$ Suggested Wine: *Turning Leaf*® *Chardonnay*   Music Selection: *Soul Food, Various Artists*

RAVIOLI STROGANOFF

Serves 4

1   20-ounce package cheese ravioli, *Rosetto's®*
1   pound lean ground turkey
1   tablespoon Italian seasoned spice blend, *McCormick®*
1   10-ounce can *Condensed Cream of Mushroom Soup, Campbell's®*
1   cup sour cream

Prep Time: 10 minutes
Cooking Time: 15 minutes

Preparation:

Preheat oven to 350 degrees. Prepare ravioli according to package directions; drain and set aside. In a medium frying pan, on medium heat, brown ground turkey with seasoned blend. Drain any fat. In a large bowl, combine cooked ground turkey, soup, and sour cream. Gently mix in ravioli. Place in a baking dish, cover and bake for 15 minutes or until thoroughly heated. Sprinkle the top with Italian seasoning. Serve hot.

$$ Suggested Wine: *Mouton Cadet® Bordeaux*   Music Selection: *Maxwell, "Embrya"*

dinner

SWEET & SOUR PORK KABOBS WITH FRIED RICE

Serves 4

1   package fried rice, *Rice-a-Roni®*
10 ounces pork loin, cubed
4   large button mushrooms
1   8-ounce can corn niblets, no salt, *Green Giant®*
1   8-ounce can peas and carrots, *Green Giant®*
1   green pepper, cut in quarters
1   red pepper, cut in quarters
4   cherry tomatoes
1   zucchini, sliced 1-inch thick
4   pearl onions (optional)
4   large skewers (soak in water for 8–10 minutes, this keeps skewers from burning)
1   4-ounce can pineapple chunks (juice to be used in marinade), *Dole®*

MARINADE:

1/3 cup sweet and sour sauce, *Dynasty®*
1/3 cup pineapple juice from canned pineapple
1   tablespoon lite soy sauce, *Kikkoman®*
1   clove garlic, minced
1   teaspoon ginger

Prep Time: 20 minutes
Cooking Time: 8–12 minutes

Preparation:

Prepare *Rice-a-Roni®* according to package instructions. Preheat broiler. In a small bowl, mix all marinade ingredients: sweet and sour sauce, pineapple juice, soy sauce, minced garlic, and ginger. Set aside. Place pork cubes in a medium bowl. In a second medium bowl, place the vegetables (mushrooms, corn niblets, peas and carrots, cut green and red peppers, cherry tomatoes, sliced zucchini, pearl onions), and pineapple. Distribute the marinade evenly between the two bowls and refrigerate for approximately 15 minutes.

Skewer the pork, vegetables, and pineapple evenly on 4 large skewers. Place on a foil-covered cookie sheet and broil for approximately 4–6 minutes. Turn each skewer over and broil for another 4–6 minutes until golden.

$$$ Suggested Wine: *Sterling Vineyards® Pinot Grigio*   Music Selection: *Celine Dion, "The French Album"*

MUSHROOM STEAK & SWEET MASH

Serves 4

4	cube steaks (approximately 4 ounces each)
1	8-ounce can cut sweet potatoes, *Princella®*
1	package mashed potatoes, *Simply Potatoes®*
1	cup all-purpose flour, *Pillsbury®*
1	cup vegetable oil, *Wesson®*
1	tablespoon salt
3	10-ounce cans beef broth, *Swanson®*
1	white onion, sliced, separated into rings
1	10-ounce can *Condensed Golden Mushroom Soup, Campbell's®*

Prep Time: 5 minutes
Cooking Time: 35 minutes

Preparation:

In a large skillet, on medium-high heat, warm oil — while warming, place flour in a large *Ziploc®* bag. Salt each cube steak generously and place in bag of flour, seal bag, and shake. Steak should be completely covered in flour. Put floured steaks in skillet and fry for approximately 5 minutes on each side. Remove steaks from oil and place on a paper towel to absorb excess oil. Using flour left over in the bag, sprinkle flour into the oil remaining in skillet (do not remove the meat's residue in skillet). Stir and cook continuously for 3–5 minutes until paste is a deep, dark color. Reduce heat to low and add beef broth. Whisk vigorously until smooth. Stir in mushroom soup. Place steaks back in skillet, making sure they're covered by the beef/mushroom gravy. Top entire skillet with onion slices (rings) and cover. Simmer for 20 minutes or until beef/mushroom gravy is thick. Add salt and pepper to taste.

While steak is simmering, warm sweet potatoes per can instructions, then mash with a fork or potato masher. Set aside in a pot on low heat to keep warm. Peel corner on *Simply Potatoes®* to remove cover. Warm potatoes according to package instructions with 1 tablespoon butter and 1/8 cup milk. On each plate, swirl mashed and sweet potatoes together and place steak on top of potatoes — smother with gravy and garnish with onion slices (rings).

$$$ Suggested Wine: *Woodbridge® Cabernet*   Music Selection: *Sting, "Nada Como El Sol"*

dinner

TROPICAL SALMON

Serves 2

12   ounces salmon tail fillet
1   tablespoon tartar sauce, *Kraft*®
2   tablespoons sour cream
1   teaspoon dijon mustard, *Heinz*®
1/4 cup dill sauce, *Lite House*®

Prep Time: 5 minutes

Preparation:

In a small bowl, combine tartar sauce, sour cream, dijon mustard, and dill sauce. Set aside for later.

RICE

1   box white rice, *Uncle Ben's*®
1   package tropical trail mix, *Delish!*®

Prep Time: 8 minutes
Cooking Time: 20 minutes

Preparation:

Preheat broiler. Prepare the rice according to the package instructions. Halfway through the cooking point, add the trail mix. This wonderful treat adds volume and texture to the rice. While the rice is cooking, cut salmon in paper-thin slices, lengthwise. Place salmon slices on glass or ceramic plates, covering half of each of the plates. Place plates under broiler for 1 minute — watch salmon carefully so it does not overcook. When finished, salmon will look pale pink and be flaky. Remove hot plates carefully. Add rice and garnish with dill sauce.

$$$ Suggested Wine: *Almaden*® *Chardonnay*   Music Selection: *Barry White, "The Icon Is Love"*

SPEEDY SWEDISH MEATBALLS

Serves 4

1   pound frozen meatballs, thawed, *Celentano*®
1   1.5-ounce package Swedish meatball gravy mix, *Schilling*®
1   cup milk
1   teaspoon celery seed, *McCormick*®
1   8-ounce package broad egg noodles, *Ronzoni*®
    vegetable oil spray, as needed, *Pam*®

Prep Time: 10 minutes
Cooking Time: 20 minutes

Preparation:

Preheat a large skillet on medium-high and spray with *Pam*®. Over high heat, brown meatballs evenly. Once all meatballs are brown, lower heat and cover. In a small pot, prepare gravy according to package instructions, using milk rather than water. Stir until smooth and add celery seed. Pour gravy over meatballs and continue to simmer for approximately 10 minutes.

Boil broad egg noodles according to package instructions. Place bed of noodles onto each plate, then top with meatballs and gravy mixture.

$$ Suggested Wine: *Sterling Vineyards*® *Merlot*   Music Selection: *Simply Red, "Greatest Hits"*

NOODLES ALFREDO

Serves 2

1	8-ounce package broad egg noodles, *Ronzoni*®
1	cup butter, *Land O Lakes*®
1	cup milk
1	cup grated parmesan cheese, *Sargento*®

Prep Time: 5 minutes
Cooking Time: 10 minutes

Preparation:

In a large pot, boil noodles according to package instructions. Drain and return to pot. Over low heat, add butter and milk to noodles and toss until combined and butter is melted. Add cheese and stir until melted. Remove from heat. Serve immediately.

$ Suggested Wine: *Straccali*® *Chianti*   Music Selection: *The London Symphony Orchestra, "Season for Love"*

DESSERTS

Like most people, I love desserts — they're my weakness. Growing up, my grandmother would make the most fabulous cakes. I would sit in the kitchen and watch her bake and decorate cakes for hours. Unfortunately, none of us has time for this luxurious expression of love anymore. To this day, I have not forgotten my grandmother's greatest creations — her famous dessert casseroles. None of us ever knew exactly what was in them, but your mouth watered in anticipation of every bite. Now I, too, have continued her not-so-common tradition. Even my grandmother would take her hat off to the wonderful desserts included here. My fabulous desserts are not as time-consuming as the old-fashion delicacies, but I promise you, they are just as amazing. Only you will know how truly easy they are to make.

Dessert

BANANA PURSE

Makes 12

3 bananas, sliced thinly
1/4 cup maple syrup, *Blackburn's®*
1 package puff pastry (2 sheets of puff pastry), *Pepperidge Farm®*
2 tablespoons milk
1 tablespoon sugar, *C&H®*
1 teaspoon cinnamon, *McCormick®*

Prep Time: 5 minutes
Cooking Time: 15 minutes

Preparation:

Preheat oven to 400 degrees. In a medium bowl, combine the bananas and syrup. Slightly mash with a fork. On a clean surface, lay flat 2 sheets of puff pastry. Cut into half, length-wise. Then into thirds, width-wise. There should be 6 squares per sheet. Evenly distribute banana mixture in the center of each square. Fold corners of the pastry into the center and pinch the ends off with a twist. Brush pillows with milk. In a small bowl, combine the sugar and cinnamon together, then sprinkle over the top of each pillow. Place on a foil-covered baking sheet that's been sprayed with nonstick spray. Bake for 15 minutes or until golden.

$$

RASPBERRY TRIFLE WITH RUM CREAM SAUCE

Serves 6

1   pound cake, thawed and cut into quarter size cubes, *Sara Lee®*
6   teaspoons raspberry jam, *Kraft®*
4   pre-made vanilla pudding cups, *Kozy Shack®*

RUM CREAM SAUCE:

1/4   stick butter, *Land O Lakes®*
1   cup powdered sugar, *C&H®*
1   teaspoon rum flavoring, *McCormick®*

Prep Time: 10 minutes
Cooking Time: 3 minutes
Set-up Time: 45 minutes

Preparation:

For Rum Cream sauce, melt butter over medium heat in a small saucepan. Whisk in powdered sugar and rum flavoring. Remove from heat and set aside. In 6 small bowls or cups, evenly distribute pound cake cubes. Pack down slightly. Evenly distribute rum sauce over each of the six cups. Add 1 teaspoon of jam to each cup and finish with 3 tablespoons of the vanilla pudding spread evenly over each. Refrigerate for 45 minutes and serve.

$$

MALIBU RUM CAKE

Makes 1 large bundt cake or approximately 8–10 servings

CAKE:

1	package yellow cake mix, *Duncan Hines*®
1	package instant vanilla pudding filling, *Kozy Shack*®
1	egg
1/3	cup oil, *Wesson*®
1 1/4	cups *Malibu Rum*®
	vegetable oil spray, *Pam*®

Prep Time: 5 minutes
Cooking Time: 30 minutes
Cooling Time: 30 minutes

Preparation:

Preheat oven to 325 degrees. In a large bowl, hand-mix yellow cake mix, vanilla pudding filling, egg, and rum until well combined. Pour into greased bundt pan and bake for 30 minutes or until knife inserted in center comes out clean. Cool for 30 minutes in the refrigerator.

GLAZE:

1	cup butter, *Land O Lakes*®
1	cup water
1	cup sugar, *C&H*®
1	cup *Malibu Rum*®

Prep Time: 3 minutes
Cooking Time: 7 minutes

Preparation:

In a medium saucepan, on medium-high heat, melt butter. Stir in water and sugar and bring to a boil. Continue to boil for 5 minutes, stirring constantly. Remove from heat and stir in rum.

Allow cake to cool. Remove cooled cake from bundt pan by turning upside down on a flat serving surface and working the sides delicately. Then top with glaze and serve.

$$

VANILLA CREAM PIE

Makes 1 nine-inch pie or 7–8 servings

1	frozen 9" pie crust, *Keebler®*
2	large bananas
8	cups pre-made vanilla pudding cups, *Kozy Shack®*
1	teaspoon vanilla extract, *Schilling®*
1	8-ounce package *Cool Whip®* (thawed)

Prep Time:	15 minutes
Cooling Time:	30 minutes
Set-up Time:	1 hour

Preparation:

Preheat oven to 375 degrees. Bake pie crust according to package instructions. Remove from oven and set aside to cool for 30 minutes. Slice bananas a quarter-inch thick and cover the bottom and sides of pie crust. In a medium bowl, mix vanilla pudding, vanilla extract, and *Cool Whip®*. Pour into pie crust and allow to chill in the refrigerator for 1 hour.

$$

$$

\$\$

BERRY COOKIE COBBLER

Serves 8

1	bag frozen mixed berry medley, or 1 12-ounce can mixed berry pie filling
1	5-ounce can of apple pie filling, *Comstock®*
1	tablespoon granulated sugar, *C&H®*
1	teaspoon cinnamon, *McCormick®*
1	roll of chunky sugar cookie dough, *Pillsbury®*

Prep Time: 4 minutes
Cooking Time: 25 minutes

Preparation:

Preheat oven to 350 degrees. In a large bowl, mix together berries, apple pie filling, sugar, and cinnamon. Pour into an 8X8X2-inch baking pan. Make small crumbles of the cookie dough over the berries, spread evenly. Cover with foil and bake for 20 minutes. Uncover and bake for an additional 5 minutes or until the cookie crust is golden and crisp. Serve warm with ice cream.

$

RICOTTA BERRY BURSTS

Serves 6

6	pastry shells, frozen, *Pepperidge Farm*®
2	tablespoons milk
2	tablespoons granulated sugar, *C&H*®

FILLING:

3	cups skim ricotta cheese
4	tablespoons boysenberry jam, *Welch's*®
2	tablespoons orange juice, *Minute Maid*®

Prep Time:	7 minutes
Cooking Time:	12 minutes
Cooling Time:	10 minutes

Preparation:

Place the pastry shells on a baking sheet. Brush each with milk and sprinkle with sugar. Then bake according to package instructions. For the filling, in a blender, combine ricotta cheese, boysenberry jam, and orange juice, and pulse conservatively until smooth. Spoon about 2+ tablespoons of the filling into each pastry shell. Serve immediately.

$$

CREAM CHEESE FLAN

Serves 8

1	cup granulated sugar, *C&H*®
1	cup water
1	12-ounce can sweetened condensed milk, *Carnation*®
1	14-ounce can evaporated milk, *Carnation*®
1	8-ounce package cream cheese, softened, *Philadelphia*®
1	cup butter, softened, *Land O Lakes*®
5	large eggs
1	teaspoon vanilla extract, *Schilling*®

Prep Time: 20 minutes
Cooking Time: 40 minutes
Cooling Time: 1 hour

Preparation:

Preheat oven to 350 degrees. Fill two large baking casserole dishes with one inch of hot water. Place 8 custard or dessert oven-safe cups in water. Combine sugar and water in a small saucepan. Cook over low heat, constantly stirring, until sugar is dissolved. Once sugar is dissolved, bring to a boil. Boil, without stirring, for 10 to 15 minutes, until liquid is golden brown. Quickly pour into cups, distributing evenly among 8. This is your flan sauce.

In a blender, combine condensed and evaporated milk, cream cheese, butter, eggs, and vanilla. Blend until smooth. Pour into cups on top of flan sauce. Place cups in baking or casserole dishes filled with water into oven. Bake for 30–40 minutes or until a butter knife inserted in the middle of a cup comes out clean. Remove cups from pan and allow to chill for at least 1 hour in the refrigerator. Serve in the cup or run a knife around the edge, invert cup, and serve with flan sauce on top.

If desired, garnish with fresh or frozen (thawed) berries.

$$

GOOEY MUD PIE

Serves 8

2	cups fat-free *Cool Whip*® (thawed)
8	cups pre-made chocolate pudding, *Kozy Shack*®
1	pint chocolate ice cream, softened, *Haagen-Dazs*®
1	chocolate pre-made pie crust, *Keebler*®
1	container chocolate *Magic Shell Topping, Smucker's*®

Prep Time:	7 minutes
Set-up Time:	1 hour

Preparation:

In a small bowl, combine *Cool Whip*® and pudding. Set aside. In a medium bowl, whip slightly thawed ice cream with an electric mixer until smooth (should have the consistency of cream cheese). Quickly spread the ice cream evenly across the bottom of the pie crust. Then add the pudding mixture on top of ice cream and top generously with chocolate *Magic Shell Topping*. Freeze for 1 hour and serve.

$$

MARBLED SOUR CREAM CAKE

Makes 1 large bundt cake or approximately 8–10 servings

1	cup semi-sweet chocolate chips, *Hershey's®*
1	package yellow cake mix, *Betty Crocker®*
4	large eggs
1	cup sour cream
1	cup vegetable oil, *Wesson®*
1	cup water
1	cup granulated sugar, *C&H®*
	vegetable oil spray, *Pam®*

Prep Time: 10 minutes
Cooking Time: 50 minutes
Cooling Time: 30 minutes

Preparation:

Preheat oven to 375 degrees. Microwave chocolate chips in a medium bowl for one minute on high. Stir and continue to microwave until chips are melted and smooth. Set aside.

To make the cake batter, in a large bowl combine yellow cake mix, eggs, sour cream, vegetable oil, water, and sugar. Mix until very well combined. Spoon 2 cups of cake batter into the melted chocolate and mix thoroughly. Alternately spoon chocolate and plain batter into a greased 9-cup bundt pan or round tube pan. Bake for 50 minutes or until a butter knife can be inserted in the middle of the cake and comes out clean. Cool for 30 minutes in the refrigerator before trying to turn pan upside down and remove cake.

If desired, garnish with fresh berries or powdered sugar.

$

KAHLUA TIRAMISU

Serves 6

1/3 cup plus 2 tablespoons Kahlua
12 lady fingers
1 8-ounce container marscapone cheese
1 tablespoon sugar, *C&H*®
6 teaspoons *Cool Whip*®, thawed
6 pre-made vanilla pudding cups, *Kozy Shack*®
1 tablespoon cocoa powder, *Hershey's*®

Prep Time: 7 minutes
Set-up Time: 30 minutes

Preparation:

In a small bowl, place 1/3 cup of Kahlua. Dip each of the lady fingers in quickly so as to just coat lightly. Then place two lady fingers against each wall of 6 very small bowls. Set aside. In a small bowl, add the marscapone, sugar, and 2 tablespoons of Kahlua. Whisk until smooth. Evenly distribute pudding mixture between the 6 bowls. Refrigerate for 30 minutes.

Top each with 1 teaspoon of Cool Whip® *and a sprinkle of cocoa just before serving.*

$$$

BANANA FOSTER'S PIE

Makes 12

5   bananas, sliced thinly
1   cup butter, softened, *Land O Lakes*®
1   cup golden brown sugar (packed), *C&H*®
2   tablespoons brandy or brandy flavoring, *Schilling*®
2   packages of 6 mini pie shells, *Keebler*®

Prep Time: 13 minutes
Cooking Time: 10 minutes

Preparation:

Preheat the oven to 400 degrees. Combine the butter and the brown sugar in a medium saucepan over medium heat. Stir until the mixture is creamy (approximately 3 minutes). Add in brandy and stir. Stir bananas into mixture. Remove from heat immediately. Let stand for 5 minutes. Place 2 tablespoons of the mixture into each pie shell. Bake pies for approximately 10 minutes or until they bubble.

Garnish: With Cool Whip® *and serve with vanilla ice cream.*

$

ABOUT YOU

about you

I would love to hear about any Semi-Homemade recipe you have come up with. Or, let me know how the Semi-Homemade Cooking technique has changed your kitchen experiences. This is all about making life easier for us all. I also encourage you to let your mind wander and explore how the Semi-Homemade philosophy can or has affected the way you decorate, garden, craft, or just relax. Beauty and fashion should also not be overlooked so be creative with your ideas.

Send your thoughts to:

Sandra Lee
Semi-Homemade Cooking
1453-A 14th Street
#126
Santa Monica, California 90404

E-mail us on our website at:
    www.semi-homemadecooking.com

I hope you enjoy this book of recipes and look forward to hearing from you soon.
s.l.

Please don't forget to include your:

Name
Address
City
State
Zip
Area Code and Home Phone
Area Code and Work Phone
E-mail Address

ABOUT YOU

I would love to hear about any Semi-Homemade recipe you have come up with. Or, let me know how the Semi-Homemade Cooking technique has changed your kitchen experiences. This is all about making life easier for us all. I also encourage you to let your mind wander and explore how the Semi-Homemade philosophy can or has affected the way you decorate, garden, craft, or just relax. Beauty and fashion should also not be overlooked so be creative with your ideas.

Send your thoughts to:

Sandra Lee
Semi-Homemade Cooking
1453-A 14th Street
#126
Santa Monica, California 90404

E-mail us on our website at:
www.semi-homemadecooking.com

I hope you enjoy this book of recipes and look forward to hearing from you soon.
s.l.

Please don't forget to include your:

Name
Address
City
State
Zip
Area Code and Home Phone
Area Code and Work Phone
E-mail Address

APPETIZERS & COCKTAILS

Social soirees can be simple, elegant, and inexpensive to pull off when you use shortcuts. I have thrown many a great party. Some for five guests, others for 50 guests, even one for 550 guests — and I can tell you, preparation and attitude are everything. Even when you're only entertaining for two — whether it's a romantic gesture or catch-up time with your best friend.

With the right combination of appetizers and cocktails, your gathering will be a guaranteed success. Good food, fun atmosphere, and a stylish presentation are always important, but they don't need to be elaborate or overwhelming to be tasteful. While everyone will appreciate all your hard work, there is no reason why they should know you *didn't* labor in the kitchen for hours.

With a little organization and simple Semi-Homemade recipes, you'll have the freedom to sit back, relax, and enjoy yourself and your guests.

APPETIZERS

COCKTAILS

SESAME CHICKEN DRUMETTES

Serves 4

1	6-ounce package frozen chicken drumettes, *Tyson®*, thawed
1	cup teriyaki sauce, *La Choy®*
1	tablespoon sherry, *E&J®*
1	tablespoon toasted sesame seeds (spice section of grocery store), *McCormick®*
1	tablespoon barbecue sauce, *KC Masterpiece®*
1	tablespoon honey, *Sue Bee®*

Prep Time: 5 minutes
Cooking Time: 25 minutes

Preparation:

Preheat oven to 400 degrees. Place thawed chicken drumettes, in a single layer, on a cookie sheet. In a small bowl, combine teriyaki sauce, sherry, and sesame seeds. Brush sauce on drumettes. Bake drumettes for 15 minutes or until golden brown, then brush them with barbecue sauce and honey and bake for another 10 minutes. Serve hot or cold.

$$

\$\$ Music Selection: *Kruder & Dorfmeister, "The K & D Sessions"*

PAN-FRIED DUMPLINGS

Serves 9 (36 dumplings)

2	8-ounce cans chow mein vegetables, *Chun King®*
2	teaspoons minced fresh garlic
1	teaspoon soy sauce, *Kikkoman®*
1	teaspoon mustard, *Heinz®*
1	teaspoon sweet and sour sauce, *La Choy®*
1	package wonton wrappers (36 count), *Star®*
1/2	cup canola oil, *Wesson®*

If desired, add meat:

1	pound cooked ground beef, pork, or chicken

Prep Time: 15 minutes
Cooking Time: 16 minutes

Preparation:

Preheat oven to 375 degrees. Drain chow mein vegetables and mince. Place in medium bowl and add garlic, soy sauce, mustard, and sweet and sour sauce and mix until well combined. (Mix meat in now if desired.) Separate wonton wrappers on a clean surface. Place a tablespoon of filling in the center of each wrapper. Top with a second wonton wrapper and seal by dampening the edges of the wrappers with cold water and pinching closed. In a saucepan, heat oil on medium-high. (When a piece of vegetable tossed into the oil bubbles and sizzles, the oil is hot enough.) Carefully fry the dumplings, turning them over so they do not stick. Fry for only 3 minutes on each side, or until beginning to brown. Place dumplings on a non-greased baking sheet and bake for 10 minutes. Serve hot, with dipping sauces (hot mustard, sweet and sour, or soy sauce).

Once cooked and cooled, dumplings can be frozen, and reheated in the oven.

$$ Music Selection: *Thievery Corporation, "Sounds from the Thievery for Life"*

CHORIZO TAQUITOS

Makes 24 pieces

16   ounces beef chorizo sausage
1   cup chunky salsa, drain, *Pace®*
1   cup shredded cheddar cheese, *Sargento®*
12   fajita-size flour tortillas, *El Paso®*
1   cup pre-made guacamole (refrigerated section), *Dean's®*
1   cup sour cream

Prep Time: 8 minutes
Cooking Time: 20 minutes

Preparation:

Preheat oven to 400 degrees. In a large skillet, sauté sausage, over medium heat, for approximately 6 minutes or until browned. Add drained salsa and cook for 2 more minutes. Set aside to cool. Once cooled, add cheese. On a clean surface, place one tortilla shell. Place a tablespoon or two of the sausage mixture into the center and distribute evenly in a straight line across the entire tortilla. Fold tortilla in half and roll like a pinwheel. Secure with toothpicks. Repeat eleven times. Place on a foil-covered baking sheet and bake for 15 to 20 minutes or until golden. Slice through the center to create two portions and serve hot with guacamole and sour cream.

$$

Music Selection: *Yo-Yo Ma, Bobby McFerrin, "Hush"*

CRABMEAT CUCUMBER ROUNDS

Makes 16 rounds

2   large unpeeled cucumbers, sliced thinly into 16 slices
1   teaspoon horseradish, *Moorehouse*®
1   teaspoon mustard, *Heinz*®
1   teaspoon Worcestershire sauce, *Lea and Perrins*®
1   tablespoon mayonnaise, *Best Foods*®
1   4.25-ounce can lump crabmeat, drained and flaked, *Chicken of the Sea*®
1   4-ounce jar sliced pimento-stuffed green olives, sliced, *Star*®

Prep Time: 15 minutes
Set-up Time: 30 minutes

Preparation:

Arrange cucumber slices in a single layer on a serving tray. Place in refrigerator until ready to use.
In a small bowl, mix together horseradish, mustard, worcestershire, and mayonnaise until well com-
bined. Add crabmeat and toss until mixed. Layer 1 tablespoon of crabmeat onto each slice of cucumber.
Garnish with olive slices. Chill at least 30 minutes before serving.

$$

Music Selection: *Amel Larrieux, "Infinite Possibilities"*

FETA-STUFFED ARTICHOKE BOTTOMS

Makes 7 pieces

2   cups jarred roasted red bell peppers, chopped, *Reese®*
4   tablespoons chopped black olives, *Red Star®*
4   tablespoons crumbled feta cheese
2   tablespoons olive oil, *Star®*
2   cans artichoke bottoms (approximately 7 pieces), *Reese®*

Prep Time: 5 minutes
Cooking Time: 5–7minutes

Preparation:

Preheat broiler. In a medium bowl, combine peppers, olives, and cheese to create the stuffing. Place artichoke bottoms on a foil-covered baking pan. Mound a spoonful of the stuffing in each artichoke. Broil for 5–7 minutes or until golden on top. Serve hot.

$$ Music Selection: *Ivy, "Apartment Life"*

ORIENTAL PORK WRAPPERS

Serves 4 (16 dumplings)

STUFFING:

1	package pork sausage, *Jimmy Dean®*
1	tablespoon lite soy sauce, *Kikkoman®*
1	tablespoon hoisin sauce, *Dynasty®*
1	clove garlic, minced
1	green onion, sliced
16	wonton wrappers, *Dynasty®*

Option: If frying, use 1 cup vegetable oil.

Prep Time: 15 minutes

Cooking Time *(based on cooking method used)*:
Steamed: 5 minutes
Fried: 4 minutes each side
Baked: 12 minutes

Preparation:

In a medium bowl, combine sausage, soy sauce, hoisin sauce, minced garlic, and sliced green onion. Lay out wontons on a clean surface and brush edges with water. Place 1 tablespoon of stuffing in the center of each wonton. Fold each wonton in a triangular shape and cook using one of the following methods.

Steaming: Place the wrappers on a collapsible metal vegetable steamer in a pan with water about 1" deep. Cover pan with lid and on high, steam for approximately 5 minutes or until cooked thoroughly. Watch the water level and add as needed.

Frying: Heat vegetable oil on medium-high heat and cook each side of wrapper for approximately 4 minutes or until cooked thoroughly.

Baking: Preheat oven to 400 degrees. Place wrappers on a foil-covered baking sheet and bake for approximately 12 minutes or until golden and cooked thoroughly.

$$ Music Selection: *Ultra Lounge, Various Artists, "Best of Collection, Volume 1"*

SMOKED SALMON & OLIVE BLINIS

Serves 8–10

6   ounces smoked salmon or lox, *Lasco® (stands for Los Angeles Seafood Co.)*
1   cup kalamata olive spread, *Peloponnese®*
1   cup non-fat sour cream

BLINIS:

1   cup buckwheat pancake and waffle mix, *Krusteaz®*

Prep Time: 5 minutes
Cooking Time: 10 minutes

Preparation:

In a medium bowl, prepare pancake mix according to package instructions. Set aside. Heat a skillet over medium heat. Spray with nonstick cooking spray. Cook several 1 tablespoon dollops of batter at a time to make blinis. Cook for 2 minutes or until bubbles appear, then turn over and cook for 1 minute. Set aside.

Place each blini on a plate, spread each with 1 1/2 teaspoons of the olive spread, top with a slice of lox, or crumble 1 teaspoon smoked salmon and finish with a teaspoon of sour cream. Serve flat or wrap it up and tie it with a blanched green onion.

$$

Music Selection: *Ultra Lounge, Various Artists "Best of Collection, Volume 11"*

ITALIAN COCONUT FONDUE

Serves 6

1   cup coconut milk (Asian food section of grocery store)
1   jar alfredo sauce, *Classico*®
1   cup white table wine, *Almaden*®
1   8-ounce can white cheese sauce, *Aunt Penny's*®
2   cups Italian blend cheeses, *Sargento*®

Prep Time: 5 minutes
Cooking Time: 8–10 minutes

Preparation:

In a nonstick saucepan, on medium heat, combine coconut milk, alfredo sauce, white wine, and white cheese sauce. Bring to a simmer. Add in Italian blend cheeses and stir until melted. Remove from heat. Serve in a fondue pot, chafing dish, or ceramic bowl.

Serve with Del Monte® whole new potatoes (cubed), French bread (cubes), Heinz® sweet midget gherkins, and figs.

FIESTA FONDUE

Serves 6

1   11-ounce can *Fiesta Nacho Cheese Soup, Campbell's®*
1   11-ounce can *Cheddar Cheese Soup, Campbell's®*
1   cup shredded cheddar cheese, *Sargento®*
10   ounces water

Prep Time: 5 minutes
Cooking Time: 8–10 minutes

Preparation:

In a nonstick saucepan, on medium heat, combine *Campbell's® Fiesta Nacho Cheese Soup, Campbell's® Cheddar Cheese Soup*, and water. Bring to a simmer. Add shredded cheddar cheese and stir until melted. Remove from heat. Serve in a fondue pot, chafing dish, or ceramic bowl.

Serve with Del Monte® whole new potatoes (cubed), French bread (cubes), Heinz® sweet midget gherkins, or figs.

$

Music Selection: *Supreme Beings of Leisure, "Self-Titled"*

WHITE CHOCOLATE FONDUE

Serves 6

I	stick unsalted butter, *Land O Lakes®*
I	package *Guittard's® Choc-au-lait Chips*
2	packages premiere white morsels, *Hershey's®*
3/4	cup heavy whipping cream

Prep Time: 3 minutes
Cooking Time: 7 minutes

Preparation:

In a nonstick saucepan, on medium heat, melt butter. Gradually add in *Choc-au-lait* and white morsel chocolate chips. Whisk continuously until smooth. Fold in the whipping cream and remove from heat. Cool slightly. Serve in a fondue pot, chafing dish, or ceramic bowl.

Serve with apples, cantaloupe, pineapple, strawberries, cookies, pretzels, Ruffles® potato chips, or pound cake cubes.

$$ Music Selection: *That Guitar Man from Central Park,* "*The People on the Hill*"

DARK CHOCOLATE FONDUE

Serves 6

1	stick unsalted butter, *Land O Lakes*®
1	package semisweet chocolate chips, *Hershey's*®
1	package real milk chocolate chips, *Hershey's*®
1	cup heavy whipping cream

Prep Time: 3 minutes
Cooking Time: 7 minutes

Preparation:

In a nonstick saucepan, on medium heat, melt butter. Gradually add in semisweet and milk chocolate chips. Stir continuously until melted and smooth. Fold in the whipping cream and remove from heat. Cool slightly. Serve in a fondue pot, chafing dish, or ceramic bowl.

Serve with apple, cantaloupe, pineapple, strawberries, cookies, pretzels, Ruffles® potato chips, or pound cake cubes.

$

Music Selection: *Various Artists, "The Wonder Years"*

BEER MARGARITAS

Serves 4

2   12-ounce bottles *Corona*® or your favorite beer
1   cup limeade, thawed, *Minutemaid*®
4   ounces tequila
1   lime cut into 4 wedges
1   egg white
1   cup table salt

Prep Time: 2 minutes

Preparation:

In a medium pitcher, combine beer, limeade, and tequila. Dip glasses in egg white and then in salt. Serve over ice in a chilled glass. Garnish with a lime wedge.

$ Music Selection: *Moby, "Play"*

RASPBERRY SAKE

Serves: 6

I   bottle (750 ml) sake, *Gekkeikan®*
I   pint (2 cups) wild raspberry juice, *Welch's®*
¹/₈ cup lemon juice, *ReaLemon®* or *Minute Maid®*
I   cup frozen raspberries, thawed
I   cup crushed ice

Prep Time: 5 minutes

Preparation:

In a blender, add sake, wild raspberry juice, lemon juice, thawed raspberries, and ice — pulse several times until raspberries are completely crushed. Strain to remove ice, place the lid on blender and store in the refrigerator until served.

$$

Music Selection: *k.d. lang, "Invincible Summer"*

GIN PLUSH

Serves 1

1 1/4 ounces gin, *Tanquerey®*
1/4 cup all nectar guava, *Kern's®*
1/4 cup pineapple juice, *Dole®*
1/4 cup orange juice (from frozen concentrate), *Minute Maid®*
1/4 cup club soda, *Canada Dry®*
4 ice cubes

Prep Time: 1 minute

Preparation: In a pint glass with a strainer, combine gin, nectar guava, pineapple juice, orange juice, club soda, and ice. Shake or stir until very cold. Strain and serve in a nice glass.

$$

SOUR APPLE MARTINI

Serves 1

1 teaspoon sweet vermouth
1 ounce apple sourball mix, *Hiram Walker®*
3/4 ounce vodka, *Smirnoff®*
4 ice cubes
1 Granny Smith apple slice

Prep Time: 1 minute

Preparation: In a pint glass with a strainer, combine sweet vermouth, apple sourball mix, vodka, and ice. Shake or stir until very cold. Strain and serve in a martini glass and garnish with the apple slice.

$$

CUBANA RUM

Serves 2

2 ounces apricot nectar, *Kern's®*
2 ounces lime juice, *Rose's®*
1 ounce apricot brandy, *E & J®*
1 ounce light rum, *Meyer's®*
1/8 cup crushed ice

Prep Time: 5 minutes

Preparation: Combine apricot nectar, lime juice, apricot brandy, light rum, and crushed ice in a blender. Pulse briefly for about 30 seconds, strain, and serve immediately in an old-fashioned glass.

$$

CHAMPAGNE PUNCH

Serves 6

2 15-ounce cans crushed pineapple, *Dole®*
1 cup lemon juice, *ReaLemon®* or *Minute Maid®*
1 cup *Curacao®*
1 cup maraschino cherry juice, *Red Star®*
1 cup dark rum, *Meyers®*
1/2 cup light brandy, *Meyers®*
1 bottle chilled champagne, *Cook's®*

Prep Time: 5 minutes
Cooling Time: 40 minutes

Preparation: In a large punch bowl or pitcher, mix *Curacao®*, cherry juice, rum, and brandy. Stir to blend. Refrigerate for 40 minutes. Just before serving, add 1 bottle of champagne. Serve immediately.

$$

Music Selection: *Bette Midler, "Bette"*

Clockwise from lower right: Gin Plush, Cubana Rum, Sour Apple Martini, Champagne Punch

SASSY SANGRIA

Makes 8 drinks

3   cups California burgundy, *Carlo Rossi*®
1   cup brandy, *Christian Brothers*®
3   tablespoons *Triple Sec*®
4   orange slices
4   lime slices
4   lemon slices
4   raspberries
1   Fuji apple, cored and diced
2   cups club soda, *Schweppes*®

Prep Time: 8 minutes

Preparation:

In a large pitcher, combine burgundy, brandy, *Triple Sec*®, orange slices, lime and lemon slices, raspberries, and apple, and refrigerate overnight. For each drink, add $^1/_4$ of the club soda to $^3/_4$ cup sangria mixture. Make sure to add pieces of all the fruit from sangria mix to each glass. Garnish with an orange slice.

$ Music Selection: *Better Than Ezra, "Deluxe"*

cocktails

SHERRY FRUIT BOWL

Serves 6

1	quart frozen strawberries, thawed
1	8-ounce can sliced peaches (with juice), *Del Monte*®
1	cup sherry or Madeira, *Christian Brothers*®
1	bottle white table wine, *Almaden*® or *Chablis*®

Prep Time: 5 minutes
Cooling Time: 1 hour

Preparation: In a punch bowl or pitcher, combine thawed strawberries, peaches, and sherry. Mix thoroughly. Refrigerate for 1 hour. Stir in white wine. Serve chilled.

$$

COOL RED WINE

Serves 6

1	cup brandy, *Christian Brothers*®
1	cup *Cointreau*®
3	cups *Almaden*® Chianti or red table wine
1/8	cup lemon juice, *ReaLemon*® or *Minute Maid*®
1/8	cup orange juice, *Minute Maid*®
1	whole orange, thinly sliced
1	cup peach slices (with juice), *Del Monte*®

Prep Time: 5 minutes

Preparation: In a chilled pitcher, combine brandy, *Cointreau*®, Chianti, lemon juice, and orange juice. Stir to mix. Add sliced orange and peaches. Serve in a wine glass. Ice cubes can be added if wine is not cold enough. Sugar can be added if not sweet enough.

$$

SCARLET O'BRANDY

Serves 2

3	ounces *Southern Comfort*®
2	ounces cranberry juice, *Ocean Spray*®
1	ounce lime juice, *Rose's*®
2	orange wedges
1	cup crushed ice

Prep Time: 2 minutes

Preparation: Combine *Southern Comfort*®, cranberry juice, and lime juice with 1 cup crushed ice. Shake well, strain, and serve immediately; garnish with an orange wedge in bucket or old-fashioned glass.

$$

BERRY SMOOTH

Serves 4

4	jiggers *Chambord*®, *Cassis Liqueur*® or *Blackberry Brandy*®
2	teaspoons lime juice, *Rose's*®
1	pint (16 ounces) chilled lemonade, *Minute Maid*®
2	cups ice

Prep Time: 3 minutes

Preparation: In a small pitcher combine *Chambord*® and lime juice. Add lemonade and 2 cups ice — stir until chilled and remove ice.

$

Music Selection: *Craig David, "Born To Do It"*

Clockwise from lower right: Sherry Fruit Bowl, Scarlet O'Brandy, Cool Red Wine, Berry Smooth

SOUPS & SALADS

Served as a snack, light lunch, side dish, or a main meal, soups and salads are always welcomed. The savviest of chefs know that soups and salads as stand-alones or as starters to a main course are foolproof ways to ensure a successful meal. There are so many varieties to choose from that few will become bored. Who doesn't love to have a fresh, crisp salad? Or a steaming bowl of flavorful soup? Both are staples of any diet.

Soups and salads are a tasty and easy way to get your daily requirements of nutrients and vitamins. They're also one of the quickest courses to create. Those of us who are watching our diets can look forward to soups and salads as satisfying, low-calorie feasts.

By adding the smallest accoutrements, you can change the flavor, texture, and presentation of your soup or salad. Something as simple as fresh toasted almonds, sweet candied walnuts, a dollop of cumin-flavored sour cream, or a decorative puff pastry piece are easy to add and a great way to show off your culinary creativity.

Soups & Salads

CRABBY BISQUE

Serves 2

1	10-ounce can restaurant-style condensed crab bisque, *Bookbinder's*® or any available kind
1	4.25-ounce can crabmeat, *Chicken-of-the-Sea*®
1	6-ounce can heavy cream
1	tablespoon fresh lemon juice, *ReaLemon*® or *Minute Maid*®
1	tablespoon chopped parsley, *McCormick*®

Prep Time: 5 minutes
Cooking Time: 6 minutes

Preparation:

In a medium saucepan, on medium heat, combine bisque, heavy cream, lemon juice, and chopped parsley. Bring to a boil. Pour equal portions into serving bowls. Garnish each with crabmeat.

$$

ROASTED PEPPER SOUP

Serves 2

1   8-ounce jar roasted bell peppers, rinsed and drained, *Mezzeta*®
2   tablespoons lite soy sauce, *Kikkoman*®
1   cup fresh orange juice, *Minute Maid*®
1   cup chicken stock, *Swanson*®
2   cloves garlic
1/4 cup sherry, *E & J*®

Prep Time: 3 minutes
Cooking Time: 5 minutes

Preparation:

In a blender, combine rinsed and drained bell peppers, soy sauce, orange juice, chicken stock, garlic, and sherry, and pulse until smooth. Place in a saucepan, and on medium heat bring to a slow boil. Season with salt and pepper.

$$

GOLDEN MUSHROOM SOUP

Serves 2

1   cup fresh portobello mushrooms
2   tablespoons olive oil, *Star®*
1   10-ounce can *Condensed Golden Mushroom Soup, Campbell's®*
1   cup heavy cream
1   teaspoon fresh minced garlic
1   cup water

Prep Time: 5 minutes
Cooking Time: 10 minutes

Preparation:

Finely mince fresh portobello mushrooms. In a small nonstick frying pan, quickly heat olive oil on medium-high and sauté mushrooms for 1 minute. Set aside. In a small pot, combine soup, cream, garlic and water. On medium-low, heat slowly, stirring to combine, until soup is hot and smooth. Add sautéed mushrooms and stir constantly for 1 minute. Serve hot. Top with a slice of mushroom right before serving.

Serve with crusty dinner rolls or garlic toast.

$$

CHEDDAR POTATO SOUP

Serves 4

1 package potatoes au gratin, *Stouffer's*®
1 jar *Cheese Whiz, Kraft*®
1 1/2 cups milk
2 tablespoons green onions, chopped
1 cup shredded cheddar cheese, *Sargento*®

Prep Time: 5 minutes
Cooking Time: 10 minutes

Preparation:

Prepare potatoes according to package directions. In a large saucepan, combine prepared potatoes, *Cheese Whiz*®, milk, and chopped onions. Bring to a boil, stirring constantly. Lower heat to medium and continue to cook, stirring, for 2 minutes. Remove from heat, ladle into serving dishes, garnish with cheese, and serve immediately.

$$

SANTE FE FIVE-BEAN SOUP

Serves 6

1   15-ounce can each of black beans, kidney beans, garbanzo beans, red beans, and navy
     (or white) beans, drained, *Del Monte*®
1   6-ounce jar chunky salsa, *Pace*®
1   10-ounce can chopped tomatoes, *Del Monte*®
1   tablespoon red pepper flakes, *McCormick*®
2   teaspoons ground cumin, *McCormick*®
1   5-ounce container sour cream
1   cup chopped onions, fresh

Prep Time: 7 minutes
Cooking Time: 20 minutes

Preparation:

Place black beans in a blender and blend until pureed. In a large sauce pot, place kidney beans, garbanzos, red beans, navy or white beans, salsa, chopped tomatoes, red pepper flakes, and cumin, stir to combine. Add pureed black beans and stir. Cover and simmer on medium-low heat for 20 minutes, stirring occasionally, until hot. Garnish with sour cream and onions.

For a smoother texture, entire soup can be pureed. Pureed soup can be chilled and used as a dip for chips, vegetables, or for a sauce to be served with rice.

$$$

CREAMY CURRIED CARROT SOUP

Serves 6

3	teaspoons or 2 cloves garlic, minced
1	small onion, chopped
1	10-ounce can sliced carrots, *Del Monte®*
4	1-ounce jars strained baby carrots (baby food section), *Heinz®*
1	10-ounce can chicken broth, *Swanson®*
1/3	cup milk
1/3	cup heavy cream
1	tablespoon curry powder, *McCormick®*
	vegetable oil spray, *Pam®*

Prep Time: 10 minutes
Cooking Time: 7 minutes

Preparation:

Spray a small frying pan with *Pam®*. On medium heat, sauté garlic and onion. In a blender, combine sliced carrots, strained baby carrots, chicken broth, milk, heavy cream, and curry powder. Blend briefly until smooth and mixed. Place in a medium saucepan, add sautéed garlic and onion, and cook over medium heat until hot. Hot soup can be garnished with fresh cilantro or chopped chilis and served with crusty bread.

Note: Soup can be chilled and served cold. Swirl sour cream or plain yogurt through the cold soup as a garnish.

$$

BAY SHRIMP & AVOCADO SALAD

Serves 2

1	8-ounce can petite peas, drained, *Green Giant®*
1	8-ounce can fresh-cut corn, drained, *Del Monte®*
1	cup shredded carrots, *Ready Pac®*
6	ounces fresh bay shrimp
3	tablespoons and 1 tablespoon champagne vinaigrette, *Girards®*
1	avocado, halved and pitted

Prep Time: 5 minutes

Preparation:

In a medium bowl, mix together peas, corn, carrots, shrimp, and 3 tablespoons dressing. Place half an avocado on each plate and equally distribute the shrimp mixture onto the avocado. Pour 1 tablespoon of dressing over each of the 2 avocado portions.

$$$

APPLE SLAW

Serves 4

1	package cole slaw mix (shredded cabbage and carrots, without sauce), *Mann's*®
1	large green apple, diced
2	tablespoons granulated sugar, *C&H*®
2	tablespoons chopped onions
1	cup sour cream
1	cup ranch dressing, *Hidden Valley*®
1	teaspoon lemon juice, *ReaLemon*® or *Minute Maid*®

Prep Time: 2 minutes
Cooling Time: 20 minutes

Preparation:

In a large bowl, toss cole slaw, diced apples, sugar, and chopped onions until combined. In a separate bowl, combine sour cream, ranch dressing, and lemon juice. Fold dressing into salad and chill for 20 minutes. Serve cold.

$$

CANDY BUTTER SALAD

Serves 4

4 tablespoons sugar (divided into 3 tablespoons and 1 tablespoon), *C&H®*
1 tablespoon Mandarin orange juice, *Minute Maid®*
1 cup halved walnuts, *Fisher Chef®*
1/4 teaspoon cinnamon, *McCormick®*

Prep Time: 5 minutes
Cooking Time: 10 minutes

Preparation:

Preheat oven to 375 degrees. In a 10-inch skillet, add 3 tablespoons sugar and Mandarin orange juice. Bring to a simmer. Add the walnuts. Cook until the sugar is absorbed and mixture starts to caramelize around the walnuts. In a small bowl, add the cinnamon and 1 tablespoon sugar. Toss the walnuts in this mixture and place on a foil-covered baking sheet. Bake in the oven for approximately 10 minutes or until walnuts appear crystallized. Set aside for later.

WISH BONE ORIENTAL SALAD

2 heads of butter lettuce, washed
1 red onion, sliced
1 8-ounce can Mandarin orange segments, *Del Monte®*

Prep Time: 3 minutes

Preparation:

On each plate, place 3–4 leaves of lettuce. Randomly place Mandarin orange segments, onion slices, and walnuts on top of each lettuce bed. Pour approximately 2 tablespoons of dressing on top of each salad and serve.

$$

EGGY POTATO SALAD

Serves 2

1   12-ounce can sliced white potatoes, room temperature, *Del Monte*®
2   tablespoons chopped onions, fresh
1   cup pickle relish, *Claussen*®
1   cup French dressing, *Kraft*®
1   ready-to-eat hard-boiled egg (available in the refrigerated or deli section), chopped
2   stalks celery, diced
1   cup mayonnaise, *Best Foods*®

Prep Time: 10 minutes
Cooling Time: 30 minutes

Preparation:

In a large bowl, toss potatoes, onions, relish, and French dressing until mixed thoroughly. Add egg, celery, and mayonnaise, and stir. Chill for 30 minutes. Serve cold.

$$

SPICY CRAB SALAD

Serves 2

1	cup cooked white rice (¹/₄ cup uncooked rice), *Minute Rice®*
1	4.25-ounce can crabmeat, *Chicken of the Sea®*
2	tablespoons sliced black olives, *Star®*
1	tablespoon sliced green olives, *Star®*
1	small tomato, diced
1	tablespoon lemon juice, *ReaLemon®* or *Minute Maid®*
3	teaspoons spice blend, *Chef Paul Cajun Magic®*
1	tablespoon red wine vinegar, *Heinz®*
1	tablespoon mayonnaise, *Best Foods®*
1	10-ounce package frozen cut asparagus, thawed and drained, *Green Giant®*

Prep Time: 5 minutes
Cooling Time: 15 minutes

Preparation:

In a large bowl, combine cooked rice, crabmeat, black and green olives, diced tomato, lemon juice, spice blend, red wine vinegar, and mayonnaise. Add asparagus and toss lightly. Cover and chill for 15 minutes or until ready to serve.

$$

PASTA GAZPACHO SALAD

Serves 4

1 20-ounce package frozen mini cheese ravioli, *Rosetto's*®
1 cup tomato sauce, *Sacramento*®
1 cup vegetable juice, *V-8*®
1 medium cucumber, peeled, seeded, and chopped
1 jar chunky salsa, *Pace*®
2 teaspoons sauce, *Tabasco*®

Prep Time: 15 minutes
Cooling Time: 30 minutes

Preparation:

Prepare ravioli according to package instructions. Drain and allow to cool. While ravioli is cooling, in a large bowl combine tomato sauce, *V-8*®, chopped cucumber, salsa, and *Tabasco*®. Add cooled ravioli to tomato sauce mixture and toss. Allow to chill for 30 minutes before serving.

$$

SNACKS

I'm a "snack-a-holic." I love to nosh. Snacking is the great American pastime, but most snacks are very fattening and unhealthy, which is why this chapter is filled with so many scrumptious, healthy tidbits that will hold you over between meals.

Most of us feel guilty about snacking between meals — however, it's been proven that eating certain foods between meals is good for us and can ultimately reduce the total amount of food that we consume. This is especially appropriate for high-energy people, people with weight issues, and growing children.

Now, enjoy noshing without guilt or concern. Healthy snacks serve many purposes. They are the perfect energy boosters for kids at the end of their school day and before homework or chores. Snacks are fun treats when bringing the family together to watch television or to play a board game. They can provide comfort on a cold winter's day and relief on a hot summer's day. Snacks are ideal to serve to friends and family who stop by and great for boosting camaraderie among co-workers at the office.

SNACKS

CARAMEL POPCORN

Serves 4

2 8-ounce bags of microwave popcorn, no salt, no butter, *Paul Newman's*®
1 pound butter, *Land O Lakes*®
1 cup brown sugar, *C&H*®
1 cup light corn syrup, *Karo*®
1 teaspoon baking soda, *Arm & Hammer*®

Prep Time: 5 minutes
Cooking Time: 30 minutes

Preparation:

Pre-heat oven to 350 degrees. Microwave popcorn and place in a large roaster pan and set aside. In a 2-quart saucepan, on medium heat, mix butter, brown sugar, and corn syrup to make caramel sauce. Add baking soda to mixture (this will cause mixture to foam, so 2-quart pan is necessary). Pour caramel mixture evenly and thinly over popcorn and stir until mixed. Place on a wax papered cookie sheet and bake for 30 minutes. Stir at least every 10 minutes. Remove from oven and break apart.

$

HEALTHY ONION RINGS

Serves 4

1	large onion		1	cup flour, *Pillsbury®*
1	cup seasoned breadcrumbs, *Progresso®*		1	large egg white, beaten
1	clove garlic, minced			vegetable oil spray, *Pam®*
1	cup low fat milk			

Prep Time: 8 minutes
Cooking Time: 30 minutes

Preparation: Preheat oven to 400 degrees. Cut onions into 1" slices. Separate sliced rings. In a small bowl, combine breadcrumbs and garlic. Set aside. Put milk, flour, and egg whites into 3 separate small bowls. Spray cookie sheet with *Pam®*. Dip each ring into milk, flour, egg white, and breadcrumbs (in that order). Place on baking sheet and bake for 30 minutes or until golden brown.

$$

CRUNCHY GARBANZO NUTS

Makes 3 cups

1	16-ounce can garbanzo beans, drained and rinsed, *Del Monte®*	2	tablespoons water
		2	tablespoons seasoned salt, *Lawry's®*
2	tablespoons soy sauce, *Kikkoman®*	1	teaspoon paprika, *McCormick®*

Prep Time: 5 minutes
Cooking Time: 30 minutes

Preparation: Preheat oven to 350 degrees. On a nonstick (or lightly greased) cookie sheet, lay out drained garbanzo beans in a single layer. In a cup, combine soy sauce, water, and spices. Sprinkle seasoning mixture over garbanzos. Bake for 30 minutes or until browned and crisped. Stir occasionally while baking to ensure even cooking. Remove from oven and serve hot or allow to cool and store in airtight container.

$

TORTELLINI & RAVIOLI BITES

Serves 4

1   6-ounce package assorted tortellini (refrigerated section), *Contadina*®
1   6-ounce package assorted ravioli (refrigerated section), *Contadina*®
¹/4   cup pesto sauce, *Contadina*®
¹/4   cup alfredo sauce, *Contadina*®
     skewers or toothpicks

Prep Time: 5 minutes
Cooking Time: 5 minutes

Preparation: Prepare tortellini and ravioli according to package instructions. Arrange both on the same plate in a decorative fashion (by color or shape). Heat the pesto and alfredo sauces separately and serve on the side. Dip tortellini and ravioli in the sauces or eat plain.

$$

HUMMUS PITAS

Serves 4

1	bag (8 pieces) pita bread, *Mr. Pita®*
1	16-ounce can garbanzo beans, drained and rinsed, *Del Monte®*
1	cup lemon juice, *ReaLemon®* or *Minute Maid®*
2	tablespoons seasoned blend, *Mrs. Dash®*
1	tablespoon parsley, *McCormick®*

Prep Time: 5 minutes
Cooking Time: 5 minutes

Preparation: Cut pita into triangles and toast in the broiler until brown and crispy. Set aside. Place garbanzo beans, lemon juice, seasoning, and parsley in a blender and blend until smooth. Serve hummus as dip with pita.

Note: Hummus can be made and stored in the refrigerator for up to 2 days.

$

MINI BISCUIT PIZZAS

Serves 6

6	ounces thinly sliced and chopped prosciutto (in deli section)
1	cup chopped onions, fresh
1	cup traditional tomato sauce, *Ragu®*
1	2-ounce can sliced mushrooms, *Green Giant®*
1	9-ounce can refrigerated buttermilk biscuits, *Pillsbury®*
1	cup shredded mozzarella (or pizza cheese blend), *Sargento®*
	vegetable oil spray, *Pam®*

Prep Time: 10 minutes
Cooking Time: 20 minutes

Preparation:

Bake biscuits according to package instructions. Set aside. Keep oven heated to 350 degrees. Spray 9-inch pie pan with *Pam®*. In a small bowl, combine prosciutto and onions. In a second bowl, combine tomato sauce and mushrooms. Slice biscuits in half and place on the bottom of the baking pan. Spread tomato mixture evenly over each biscuit. Then add mozzarella. Top with prosciutto and onions. Bake for 10 minutes or until cheese is golden brown. Serve hot.

$$

BUTTERSCOTCH FUDGE CRISPS

Makes 3 dozen cookies

1	cup semi-sweet chocolate chips, *Hershey's*®
1	cup butterscotch baking chips, *Hershey's*®
1	1.5-pounds package chocolate chunk brownie mix, *Betty Crocker*®
1	egg

Prep Time: 12 minutes
Cooking Time: 10 minutes

Preparation: Preheat oven to 350 degrees. Place $3/4$ cup chocolate chips and $3/4$ cup butterscotch chips together in a microwave-safe bowl, and microwave for one minute on high. Stir and continue to microwave until melted and smooth. In a large bowl, prepare brownies according to package instructions (includes an egg), using only one-half the water listed. Stir in melted chips. Stir in remaining hard chips. Place medium-size spoonfuls of dough 2" apart on a nonstick cookie sheet. Bake for 10 minutes.

$$

APPLE GRAPENUTS® CHEWS

Makes 3 dozen pieces

2   large egg whites, beaten until foamy
1   8-ounce jar sweetened applesauce, *Mott's®*
1   cup apple juice concentrate, thawed, *Mott's®*
1   cup banana bread mix, *Betty Crocker®*
1   cup cereal, *Grapenuts®*

Prep Time: 7 minutes
Cooking Time: 10 minutes

Preparation: Preheat oven to 400 degrees. In a large bowl, mix egg whites, applesauce, and apple juice concentrate together. In a small bowl, combine banana bread mix and *Grapenuts®*. Add applesauce mixture to dry ingredients and stir until completely combined. Drop 1 tablespoon every 1 inch onto a non-stick cookie sheet. Bake for 8–10 minutes or until golden brown.

$$

BAGEL CHIP DIP

Serves 6

1	16-ounce container sour cream
1	2/3 cups mayonnaise, *Best Foods*®
2	teaspoons dill weed
2	teaspoons seasoned salt, *Lawry's*®
2	teaspoons parsley flakes
1	cup chopped onion
2	bags of bagels, cut into bite-size pieces

Prep Time: 5 minutes

Preparation: In a medium bowl, mix sour cream, mayonnaise, dill weed, salt, parsley flakes, and chopped onions until smooth. Serve dip with bite-sized bagels.

$

STUFFED CRESCENTS

Serves 6

6   crescent rolls, *Pillsbury®*
1   cup shredded cheddar cheese, *Sargento®*
1   cup parmesan cheese (grated), *Kraft®*
1   4.4-ounce jar onion-flavored cheese spread, *Boursin®*

Prep Time: 5 minutes
Cooking Time: 15 minutes

Preparation: Preheat oven to 350 degrees. Lay crescent dough flat on a clean surface. Fill 2 rolls with cheddar cheese, 2 rolls with parmesan cheese, 2 rolls with onion cheese spread. Roll up dough to secure filling and place on baking sheet. Bake for approximately 15 minutes or until cooked thoroughly and golden on top. Cut each roll in half and serve hot.

$$

BURSTING BLUEBERRY SNACKS

Serves 8 (makes 16 muffins)

2	cups frozen blueberries, thawed, *Comstock®*
I	cup pitted dates, *Sunmaid®*
I	cup *Grapenuts®*
2	large, ripe bananas, sliced
I	cup raisins, *Dole®*

Prep Time: 6 minutes
Set-up Time: 3 hours

Preparation:

In a blender, place blueberries and pulse for 1 minute, add dates gradually in between pulsing (so dates don't stick to blades). In custard dishes or glass bowls, add *Grapenuts®* to line bottom and fill each halfway with blueberry mixture. Place sliced bananas on top of mixture and sprinkle with raisins. Cover with remainder of blueberry mixture. Refrigerate for 1 hour.

$$

$$

GRAVIES & SAUCES

Have you ever wondered how to change the flavor of an ordinary meal? How about fixing the taste of something you overcooked? Are you bored with meatloaf and pasta? Does one more night of "rubber chicken" make you want to go squawking out of the kitchen? Before you fly the coop, you should know that I am an expert at livening up those old standbys. What is the answer? Gravies and Sauces. Many people find making a gravy or sauce to be a challenge. But I have learned it's the easiest thing to do with a little know-how. My family lovingly dubbed me the "Gravy Queen." I can show you how to camouflage any imperfection, whether it's in presentation or taste.

I will share with you the secrets to giving the old food you fancy a new flavor. Whether you are serving red meat, fish, poultry, or pasta, you'll always find a recipe that will make any dish delicious.

Gravies & Sauces

GRAVIES & SAUCES

CREAMY MUSTARD SAUCE

Makes 1 1/2 cups

1   cup mustard, *Heinz®*
1/8   teaspoon white pepper, *McCormick®*
1   cup heavy cream
1   tablespoon lemon juice, *ReaLemon®* or *Minute Maid®*

Prep Time: 5 minutes
Cooking Time: 10 minutes

Preparation:

In a small saucepan, combine mustard, pepper, and heavy cream. Cook over low heat, stirring constantly until hot. Add lemon juice and simmer for 2 minutes. Serve immediately.

Serve over pork, ham, steamed vegetables, potatoes, or rice.

$

EASY PESTO

Makes 1 1/2 cups

1 1/2 cups fresh basil leaves
3   tablespoons fresh minced garlic
1   cup pine nuts
1   cup grated parmesan cheese, *Kraft®*
1   cup olive oil, *Star®*

Prep Time: 5 minutes
Cooking Time: 3 minutes (microwave)

Preparation: Place basil leaves, garlic, and pine nuts into blender. Pulse until paste is formed (about 1 minute). Add cheese and olive oil and pulse until mixture is smooth. Place in microwave-safe bowl and heat on medium for 2 minutes or until hot. Serve immediately.

Serve over chicken, veal, seafood, or pasta.

$$

MORE THAN MEATLOAF GRAVY

Makes 1 1/2 cups

2   tablespoons canola oil, *Heartlight®*
2   tablespoons all-purpose flour, *Pillsbury®*
1   10-ounce can beef broth, *Swanson®*
1   tablespoon meatloaf gravy mix, *Schilling®*
2   teaspoons tomato puree, *Hunts®*

Prep Time: 2 minutes
Cooking Time: 10 minutes

Preparation: In a medium frying pan, on medium heat, warm oil. Add flour and stir to form a paste. Let paste cook until it's a deep golden brown. Add beef broth, gravy mix, and tomato puree and stir. Reduce heat to low and simmer for 5 minutes or until hot and bubbly.

Serve over meatloaf, meatballs, beef, veal, potatoes, or rice.

$

SHERRY MUSHROOM GRAVY

Makes 2 cups

1   tablespoon softened butter, *Land O Lakes®*
1   tablespoon sherry, *E & J®*
2   tablespoons all-purpose flour, *Pillsbury®*
1   8-ounce can sliced mushrooms, drained, *Green Giant®*
1   cup milk, heated

Prep Time: 5 minutes
Cooking Time: 10 minutes

Preparation: Place butter, sherry, flour, and mushrooms in a blender. Pulse until mushrooms are pureed. Add milk and pulse until smooth. Pour mixture into a small saucepan and warm on medium heat stirring constantly until hot and bubbly.

Serve over steaks, chops, beef, turkey or veggie burgers, omelets, potatoes, or rice.

$$

Clockwise from lower right: Sherry Mushroom Gravy, Easy Pesto, More than Meatloaf Gravy

RICOTTA CHIVE SAUCE

Makes 2 cups

1	10-ounce can *Cream of Chicken Soup, Campbell's®*
3	tablespoons ricotta cheese
	(or small curd cottage cheese)
1	teaspoon nutmeg, *McCormick®*
1	tablespoon chopped chives (dried), *Schilling®*
1	cup chicken broth, *Swanson®*

Prep Time: 2 minutes
Cooking Time: 5 minutes

Preparation: In a blender, place cream of chicken soup, ricotta cheese, nutmeg, chopped chives, and chicken broth. Pulse until smooth. Pour into medium saucepan and warm on medium-low heat, stirrring constantly until sauce is hot and bubbly.

Serve over noodles, rice, potatoes, or vegetables.

$$

VEGETABLE CREAM SAUCE

Makes 1 1/2 cups

1	10-ounce can cream soup, *Campbell's®*
	(try broccoli, asparagus, potato, or celery)
1	cup milk
1	cup shredded pizza cheese, *Sargento®*
1	tablespoon chopped fresh parsley
1	teaspoon dried dill, *McCormick®*

Prep Time: 2 minutes
Cooking Time: 5 minutes

Preparation: In a small saucepan, on medium heat, combine cream soup and milk. Stir constantly until hot. Slowly add cheese, stirring until it's melted. Add chopped parsley and dill, simmer for 3 minutes and serve hot.

Serve over pasta, rice, couscous, vegetables, or potatoes.

$$

BLENDED HOLLANDAISE SAUCE

Makes 1 pint

6	large egg yolks
2	tablespoons lemon juice, *ReaLemon®* or *Minute Maid®*
1	teaspoon cayenne, *McCormick®*
1	cup butter, melted and hot, *Land O Lakes®*

Prep Time: 4 minutes

Preparation: In a blender, place yolks, lemon juice, and cayenne. Pulse for 10 seconds. Add butter and pulse for 10 seconds. Place mixture in a small saucepan over low heat and keep warm until served. Serve immediately or keep warm on top of stove.

Note: When working with eggs, be certain to keep them cold until used.

Serve over beef, chicken, turkey, vegetables, omelets, rice, or potatoes.

$$

Clockwise from lower front: Blended Hollandaise Sauce, Ricotta Chive Sauce, Vegetable Cream Sauce

HERBED TOMATO SAUCE

Makes 1 1/2 cups

1	8-ounce jar tomato sauce (any flavor), *Classico*®
1	4-ounce container sour cream
1	tablespoon Italian seasoned spice blend, *McCormick*®

Prep Time: 3 minutes
Cooking Time: 5 minutes

Preparation: In a medium saucepan, combine tomato sauce, sour cream, and seasoned blend. Stir over medium heat for 5 minutes or until well combined and hot.

Serve over pasta, rice, vegetables, or potatoes.

$

GARLIC CHICKEN GRAVY

Makes 1 1/2 cups

3	tablespoons butter or margarine, *Land O Lakes*®
3	tablespoons all-purpose flour, *Pillsbury*®
1	cup milk
1	cup chicken broth, *Swanson*®
2	teaspoons garlic powder, *McCormick*®

Prep Time: 3 minutes
Cooking Time: 8 minutes

Preparation: In a medium frying pan, on medium heat, melt butter or margarine. Stir in flour to form a paste. Whisk in milk and broth until smooth. Add garlic powder and reduce heat to low. Let simmer for 5 minutes. Serve hot.

Serve over chicken, turkey, seafood, potatoes, or rice.

$

Clockwise from lower right: Garlic Chicken Gravy, Herbed Tomato Sauce, Green Pepper Steak Gravy, Horseradish Sour Cream Sauce

GREEN PEPPER STEAK GRAVY

Makes 2 cups

1	tablespoon canola oil, *Heartlight*®
1	cup frozen chopped bell pepper, thawed, *Green Giant*®
2	cups beef broth, *Swanson*®
1	cup flour, *Pillsbury*®
1	teaspoon mustard, *Heinz*®

Prep Time: 3 minutes
Cooking Time: 7 minutes

Preparation: In a medium frying pan, on medium heat, warm oil. Sauté pepper until soft. Add broth and allow to come to a simmer. In a small bowl, combine flour with 1 cup of hot broth and whisk until flour is completely dissolved. Slowly pour flour mixture into rest of broth, whisking vigorously; continue to cook and whisk until mixture is smooth. Stir in mustard until dissolved. Reduce heat to low and allow to simmer for 3 more minutes.

Serve hot over beef, veal, pork, duck, turkey, potatoes, or rice.

$

HORSERADISH SOUR CREAM SAUCE

Makes 1 1/2 cups

1	8-ounce container sour cream
1	cup milk
1	tablespoon horseradish (also called creamed horseradish), *French's*®
1	teaspoon mustard, *Heinz*®
1	teaspoon white pepper, *McCormick*®

Prep Time :   2 minutes
Cooking Time: 8 minutes

Preparation: In a medium saucepan, on medium heat, combine sour cream and milk. Stir constantly while heating. Add horseradish, mustard, and white pepper and stir. Reduce heat to low and let simmer for 5 minutes or until sauce is hot.

Serve over potatoes, vegetables, seafood, or beef.

$

index

INDEX

music & wines

music

wines